ADOBE PHOTOSHOP 2025

USER GUIDE

THE COMPREHENSIVE BEGINNER TO EXPERT ILLUSTRATIVE MANUAL TO MASTERING ADOBE PHOTOSHOP 2025 WITH UPDATED SHORTCUTS, TIPS & TRICKS

PETER JOHN

TABLE OF CONTENT

INTRODUCTION

Adobe Photoshop 2025 User Guide is here. This book aims to teach you everything there is to know about the most widely used image editing programs worldwide. This book will help you become an expert Photoshop user and produce amazing images, covering everything from the fundamentals to more complex techniques.

A powerful tool that can be used for many different tasks is Adobe Photoshop. These tasks include photography, digital arts, graphic design, video editing, etc.

Photoshop can be used for a multitude of photo editing tasks, including cropping, resizing, adjusting brightness and colors, and eliminating blemishes.

Photoshop can be used for graphic design, which includes making graphics for print, social media, and websites.

Photoshop is a tool that can be used to produce concept art, paintings, and drawings.

Regardless of your degree of experience, there is something for you to learn from this book. You will learn the fundamentals of image editing, including how to use layers, masks, and filters, if you are a beginner. You will learn advanced techniques like color correction, compositing, and photo manipulation if you are an experienced user.

CHAPTER ONE

ADOBE PHOTOSHOP`S FEATURE OVERVIEW

The Adobe Photoshop software application was developed by Adobe Inc. and made available for Windows and macOS. Photoshop was developed in 1987 by the American brothers Thomas and John Knoll, and in 1988 they sold the distribution rights to Adobe Inc. Since then, the program has developed into the industry standard for all types of digital art, including manipulating raster graphics.

The fact that Photoshop has changed over the years—from version 0.07 to Photoshop CS, Photoshop CC, and finally to Photoshop 2025(Version 26)—is undisputed.

New and Updated Features in Photoshop 2025

✦ **Distraction Removal Tool**: Organize your scene with a single click. The Remove tool's Distraction Removal feature automatically finds and eliminates background objects like wires and people.

✦ **Remixing Photographs:** With just a few clicks, you may change backgrounds and fix defects. Change someone is expression, add effects, and experiment with color. You may rapidly achieve the desired style for your images with the help of powerful editing tools.

✦ **Generate Background**: You can remove and replace the background of an image using AI-generated content based on the prompts sent. This tool allows you to quickly add fresh backgrounds. To replace your scenery with a fresh one that complements your subject, use Generate Background.

✦ **Generate Workspace for Ideation**: This new workspace is designed for batch generation and allows for easy application of effects across multiple images quickly.

✦ **Combine Photos**: Parts of photos can be clipped out using selection tools, then rearranged to produce a completely new composite.

✦ **Next Gen-Fill**: With the power of the most recent Adobe Firefly Image Model, you can create images that are richer and more photorealistic using the most sophisticated Generative Fill yet.

The Minimum and Recommended Requirements of Photoshop 2025

Verify whether Adobe Photoshop 2025 is compatible with your Mac or Windows machine before downloading and installing it. The fact that this software currently has some updated and advanced capabilities is another reason to check if your Mac and Windows computers can utilize it.

To run and utilize Photoshop, your computer must fulfill the minimal requirements listed below.

For Windows

	Minimum	Recommended
Processor	Multicore processors from AMD, WinARM, or Intel®	
Operating system	Win 11 (V21H2, V22H2, V23H2, V24H2); Win 10 (V22H2)	
RAM	8 GB	16 GB or more
VRAM	1.5 GB	2 GB
Graphics card	• GPU running DirectX 12 (at least feature level 12_0) • GPU memory of 1.5 GB	• GPU that supports DirectX 12 (at least feature level 12_0)

	• GPU less than seven years old. Provide drivers with the most recent information from the manufacturer's website. GPUs that are more than seven years old are not tested by Adobe.	• 4 GB of GPU memory for screens larger than 4K
Monitor resolution	Supported colour formats include 8, 16, and 32-bit; 100% scaling for 1280 x 800 or 150% scaling for 1920 x 1080.	At least a 1920 x 1080 display
Hard disk space	10 GB of available hard disk space	100 GB of available hard disk space • Fast internal SSD for app installation • Separate internal drive for scratch disks
Internet	Access to online services, subscription verification, and essential program activation require internet connection and registration.	
Processor	ARM processor	
AVX	CPUs with AVX2 Compatibility from AMB or Intel	
SEE	Platforms from AMD or Intel that enable SS 4.2 or higher	
Operating system	Windows 10 ARM device running Windows 10 64-bit (version 20H2) or later	
RAM	8 GB	16 GB or more

Graphics card	4 GB of GPU memory	

Every other specification for ARM also applies to INTEL

For macOS

	Minimum	Recommended
Processor	Apple Silicon or Intel® multicore processor	Apple Silicon processor based on ARM
Operating system	macOS versions 12*, 13, 14, and 15	You cannot install macOS Sonoma (version 14.6.1) on macOS v11.x (Big Sur) or lower.
RAM	8 GB	16 GB or more
Graphics card	• GPU with Metal support • 1.5 GB of GPU memory	• Metal-supporting GPU • 4 GB of GPU memory or more for 4K displays
Monitor resolution	Supported color formats include 8-, 16-, and 32-bit; 1024 x 768 or higher	At least a 1920 x 1080 display
Hard disk space	10 GB of available hard disk space	100 GB of available hard disk space • Fast internal SSD for app installation

		• Additional high-speed drive(s) or SSD to set up scratch disk
	Installing Photoshop won't work on a volume with a case-sensitive file system.	
Internet	Access to online services, membership verification, and essential software activation require internet connection and registration.	
Processor	ARM-based Apple Silicon processor	
SSE	Platforms from AMD or Intel that enable SSE 4.2 or higher	
AVX	CPUs with AVX2 Compatibility from AMB or Intel	
Operating system	macOS Big Sur (version 11.2.2) or later	
RAM	8 GB	16 GB or more

Downloading & Installing Photoshop 2025

Downloading Photoshop 2025

Follow the instructions below to successfully download Photoshop 2025

- ↕ On your web browser, enter the URL link below to download Photoshop 2025:
  https://filecr.com/windows/adobe-photoshop-2025/?id=013648900000
  Carefully read through the instructions that are present on the website page
- ↕ Click on **Direct Download**.

➤ You will be opened up to a new tab, click on **Download** to download Photoshop 2025 Setup on your PC.

Thanks for Downloading

Adobe Photoshop

⊙ Click to Download

The password for Zip file is: 123

For more help please visit Faqs

Installing Photoshop 20255
After you have successfully downloaded Photoshop 2024, follow the procedures below to install it on your PC.

➤ Extract the Photoshop software application from its encoded file format using WINRAR and extract it to the desired location of your choice on your PC.

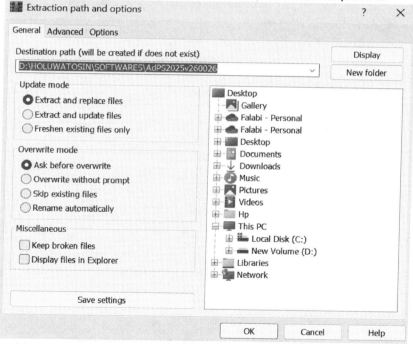

➤ Open the extracted folder, open the **DISC file**

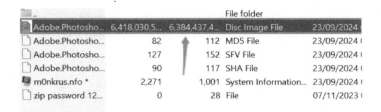

			File folder		
Adobe.Photosho...	6,418,030,5...	6,384,437,4...	Disc Image File	23/09/2024
Adobe.Photosho...	82	112	MD5 File	23/09/2024
Adobe.Photosho...	127	152	SFV File	23/09/2024
Adobe.Photosho...	90	117	SHA File	23/09/2024
m0nkrus.nfo *	2,271	1,001	System Information...	23/09/2024
zip password 12...	0	28	File	07/11/2023

- Open a folder named "**PSE 2025**".

			File folder		
Autoplay	1,958,046	1,958,046	File folder	20/09/2024 11:...
PSE 2025	6,415,316,8...	6,415,316,8...	File folder	20/09/2024 11:...
autoplay.exe	189,808	189,808	Application	05/08/2008 19:...
autorun.inf	70	70	Setup Information	05/10/2020 07:...
m0nkrus.nfo	2,271	2,271	System Information...	22/09/2024 21:...

- Select the Setup File and open it.

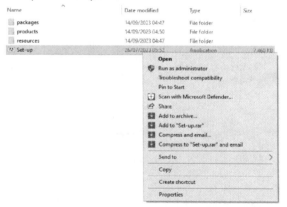

- Follow the instructions displayed on your screen to the end to successfully install Photoshop 2025 on your PC.

8

♦ After installing Photoshop on your PC. Launch it and a preview will appear on your screen like the one below. This means that Photoshop has been successfully installed and running.

CHAPTER TWO

GETTING FAMILIAR WITH PHOTOSHOP'S WORKSPACE

What you will learn in this chapter.

- **How to make the most of Photoshop's home screen and other workspaces.**
- **Working with the Menu Bar Choosing and utilizing Photoshop's tools.**
- **Using a panel efficiently and opening the panel docks.**

Working With the Home Screen

The Home Screen is the first thing that appears on the interface when the Photoshop application is activated. Your Home Screen arrangement is personalized based on your Photoshop skills and Creative Cloud subscription plan. Your home screen will look blank because you haven't done anything on it yet, but your most recent works will eventually appear there. To go back to the home screen while working on a Photoshop document, click the **Home** icon in the Options bar. To exit the home screen, just use the **Esc** key.

When Photoshop is opened, the Home screen displays the following.:

✦ **Photoshop Logo**: It can be found directly beneath the Menu Panel. When you click the logo, the default workspace appears..

✦ **Menu Panel**: File, Edit, Image, Layer, Type, Select, Filter, 3D, View, Plugins, Window, and Help are among the options in the Menu panel, which is situated in the top-left corner of the home screen. You can easily and quickly access all of these features when using Photoshop.

✦ A range of tutorials, including practical tips, to help you quickly learn and understand the concepts, ideas, and processes available in Photoshop.

10

⬧ Your home screen's **Recents** section will display and make available any documents you've recently accessed or shared with others in the cloud. You can also filter cloud documents using a keyword. Cloud documents that are only available online will appear greyed out, but you can still filter them with a keyword when offline.

⬧ **New File**: When starting a new document for a project, you click on this button. As seen below.

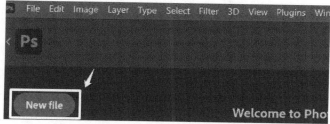

⬧ **Open**: You can open files from your computer's storage or cloud storage by clicking on this button.

⬧ **Home**: To access the Home screen, click this tab.

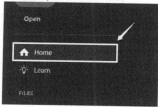

✦ **Learn**: To get started with Photoshop, click this tab to view a range of beginner's and expert tutorials.

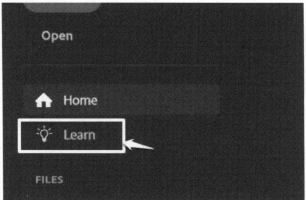

✦ **Files**: There are four parts in this area of the home screen. **Your Files, Shared With You, Lightroom Photos**, and **Deleted**. Without first logging into Cloud Creative, you cannot access this section.

✦ The files that are synced with your creative cloud storage are referred to as "**Your Files.**"

✦ **Shared With You**: These are files that coworkers, designers, etc. have given you access to.

✦ **Lightroom Photos**: This allows you to access and import synched images from Adobe Lightroom.

✦ **Deleted**: This section contains files that you have deleted from your creative cloud. This is Photoshop's recycling bin option.

Photoshop Workspaces

Panels, bars, and windows are just a few of the elements that make up the Photoshop workspace. These elements are used to create and work with projects, data, and images. By creating your own workspace or selecting from a variety of preset workspaces, Photoshop may be tailored to your workflow. The workspace is the user interface of Photoshop.

When you open an existing file or create a new one, a workspace automatically appears on your screen..

The workspace in Photoshop is made up of the following main components:

- ◆ **Drawing Canvas**: It serves as the canvas board upon which your projects and images are displayed. Below is a drawing canvas displaying a project.

♦ **Menu Bar**: Located at the top of the workspace, it contains doors that lead to some important features/commands on Photoshop. These doors are **File**, **Edit**, **Image**, **Layer**, **Type**, **Select**, **Filter**,**3D**, **Plugins**, **View**, **Window**, and **Help**.

These doors further contain submenus for relevant items. *For instance, **Windows** allows you to change your workspace and its contents.*

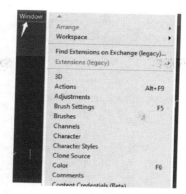

✦ **Tool Panel**: The Tools area contains tools for creating and modifying images, artwork, page elements, and more. On the left side of your workstation is this panel.

There is a grouping of related tools. *For instance, the Move Tool and the Artboard Tool are grouped in the Move Tool. Right-click your mouse to access the contents of a grouped tool.*

✦ **Option Bar**: Options (other controls) for the presently selected tool are shown in the Options bar. It is located right below the Menu Bar. *The image below is the option bar for the Brush Tool.*

✦ **Panels**: You can track and edit your work with the help of the Panels. *Below is the Properties Panel.*

15

Panels may be docked, stacked, or clustered together.

- **Rulers**: The Ruler tool is extremely useful when trying to find precise distances between two spots to correct photographs. Use Ctrl/Command + R to display your rulers.

Working with The Workspace

Because it is multifunctional and a basic workspace that is often seen as more useful and practical, Photoshop's Essentials workspace is the default workspace. We can choose which panels will be shown in our workspace and arrange the Photoshop toolbar. Keyboard shortcuts and customizable menus are also features of workspaces. The Photoshop layout is easily customizable to fit our preferred working methods and certain tasks. Photoshop offers a wide variety of panels, such as brushes, channels, layers, masks, and more.

Among the many workspaces that Photoshop comes with by default are those for 3D, design, motion, painting, graphics, and photography. Photoshop contains a lot of panels, therefore it's not a good idea to have them all visible in your workspace. To choose the workstation of your dreams.

- Select the **Window** Menu and click **Workspace**
- From the Workspace Menu, pick the workspace of your choice. **Essential** is a good workspace for beginners.

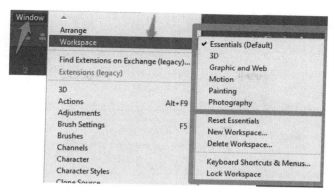

You have control over how the toolbar is displayed and how the panels that show up in your workspace are arranged. Workspaces can have their menus and keyboard shortcuts altered. You may quickly alter the Photoshop layout to suit specific activities and your preferred working style. Photoshop includes a wide variety of panels, including brushes, channels, layers, masks, and more.

To add a panel to your workspace, follow the procedure below,

- Select **Windows** in the **Menu bar**
- A series of panels are displayed, Pick the panel of your choice and it displays automatically on your screen.
- You can either add your panes to your **Panel Dock** or anywhere you desire.

Do the following to reset your workspace.

- ✦ Select **Windows** in the **Menu bar** and select **Workspace** from the drop-down menu.

- ✦ Select **Reset Essentials** from the drop-down menu.

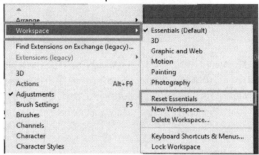

Do the following to create a new Workspace.

- ✦ Be sure your panels, toolbar, and other tabs are arranged the way you need them to be.
- ✦ Select **Windows** in the **Menu bar** and select **Workspace** from the drop-down menu.

- ✦ Select **New Workspace** from the drop-down menu.

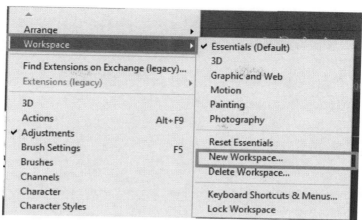

✦ Name your new workspace and select Save.

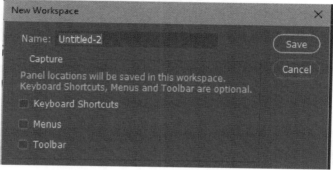

Do the following to delete a workspace.

✦ Make sure that the workspace you desire to delete is not currently opened.
✦ Select **Windows** in the **Menu bar** and select **Workspace** from the drop-down menu.

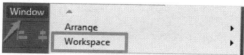

✦ Select **Delete Workspace** from the drop-down menu.

19

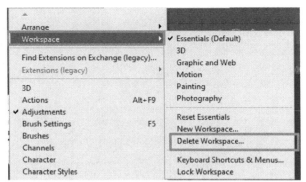

✦ From the menu preview that pops up on the screen, select the workspace you want to delete and click on **Delete**.

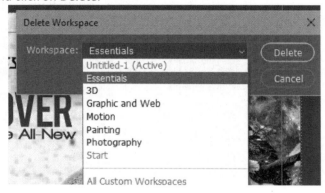

The Contextual Taskbar

The contextual taskbar Quick Command taskbar appears on your workspace when you launch your Photoshop. It contains some quick commands such as *Select Subject* and *Remove Background*.

Click on the three dots at the right side of the bar to edit your taskbar.

- Selecting *More Properties* takes you to the *Properties Panel*
- *Hide bar* hides the contextual taskbar
- **Reset bar position** allows you to change the position of the taskbar.
- *Pin bar position* allows you to pin the taskbar on a fixed position.

Working with The Menu Bar

The menu bar, which sits at the top of Adobe Photoshop, is one of its main components. The menu bar can be used to open and save files, change the canvas's size, launch and exit windows, and access other editing tools.

The menu bar has 12 options: File, Edit, Image, Layer, Type, Select, Filter, 3D, View, Plugins, Window, and Help. Under each of the main menus are additional submenus for pertinent things. Most of the menu bar's components are also accessible via keyboard shortcuts, right-click menus, or particular menus within other windows, such as Tools, Layers, Timeline, etc. You have to use the menu bar for certain settings, though. Let's quickly go over each of the options in the menu bar shown below.

File: The File menu in Photoshop is quite similar to the File menu in other programs. It is the primary tool for opening, saving, printing, and creating new files.

For example, if you've just opened Photoshop and want to import a PNG or JPG file, you can use the File menu to select **Open** and examine the image you wish to use. Advanced open actions are also enabled, such as exporting to a video format, storing photos for online use to reduce their size, and opening smart objects. The File menu's **Open Recent** option displays the ten most recently opened files. If you haven't moved the original file elsewhere, you can use that option to rapidly reopen a file without having to go through the usual "open, select, browse" routine.

The File menu is where you may also convert a video.

Edit: The Edit menu allows you to modify objects on the canvas, shortcuts, menu items, and more.

For example, you can simply undo or redo a recent activity, or you can cut, copy, and paste. Because those are common tasks, you'll utilize those menu choices a lot, or at the very least learn their keyboard shortcuts.

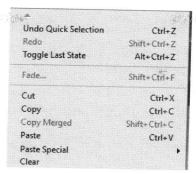

You may edit with text and selections by using the Edit menu, which allows you to look for and swap out specific words and phrases in a document. You can also decide to **Add A Stroke** along a selected path or **Fill Selections**.

Tools for object transformation are also available here. To determine whether you want to warp, rotate, scale, distort, or flip an image, use the **Edit > Transform submenu**. This section may also have the Free Transform tool, which lets you alter the height, width, and orientation.

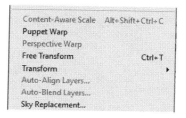

To see brushes, gradients, swatches, and custom shapes, and load your custom ABR brushes, launch Preset Manager from the Edit menu.

23

To modify RGB, CMYK, and other color profiles, you can also open Color Settings (and also load custom CSF and PSP files). The Sky replacement feature, content-aware scale, and many others are also accessible in the Edit menu.

This menu is used to find already-existing keyboard shortcuts, define new ones, modify general Photoshop preferences, and show/hide which items are displayed on the menu bar.

Keyboard Shortcuts...	Alt+Shift+Ctrl+K
Menus...	Alt+Shift+Ctrl+M
Toolbar...	
Preferences	

Image: Under the Image menu in Photoshop, there are a lot of choices for altering photos.

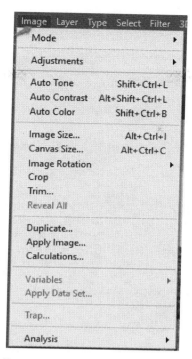

The first submenu, Mode, allows you to change the mode of the entire canvas. Modes such as RGB, greyscale, CMYK, multichannel, duotone, and others are available for selection.

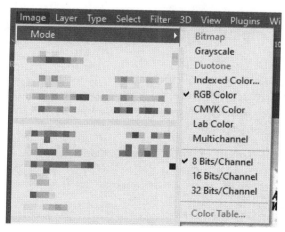

The **Adjustments** submenu is the next, and it provides access to several tools for adjusting an image's brightness, contrast, levels, exposure, Vibrance, hue/saturation, and color balance. The tools for the Photo Filter, Channel Mixer, and Color Lookup are all included here as well.

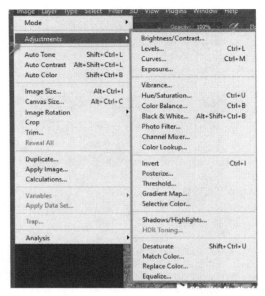

With the Auto Tone, Auto Contrast, and Auto Color choices, adjustments can be made to an image's appearance without using menus or sliders.

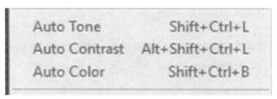

The **Image Size** and **Canvas Size** settings in the Image menu are helpful tools for working with Canvas. The Canvas Size option would be used to adjust the size of the canvas or to make the entire working area the exact size that is required. Rotating images is possible using the image menu's **Image Rotation** feature.

The Crop and Trim tools on this menu are also significant. The first step is to manually select which areas should be removed to resize the canvas. The second option removes transparent or preset-color pixels from any canvas edge to automatically resize.

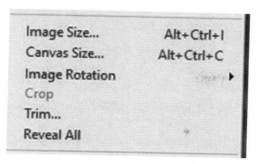

Image Size...	Alt+Ctrl+I
Canvas Size...	Alt+Ctrl+C
Image Rotation	▶
Crop	
Trim...	
Reveal All	

Layer: Among other things, the Layer menu allows you to add new layers, duplicate existing ones, and remove and rename layers. This menu also offers options for adding fill layers, adjustment layers, and layer masks.

For example, clicking on a fill layer creates a new layer that is already filled with the gradient, pattern, or color of your choice. The Layer menu also allows you to create and modify Smart Objects, export their contents, and swap them out for those of other Smart Objects. You can also link and merge layers, group and hide layers, lock layers, place layers in front of or behind other layers, flatten the image to automatically merge all the layers, and group and hide layers using other choices in the Layer menu.

Type: In Adobe Photoshop, the first "Type" choice is "Panels." This option's fly-out menu displays many sets of options. These are:

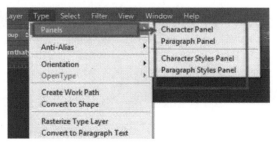

✦ Character Panel is like an extended version of the options bar after you select the type tool.

- Paragraph Panels: this is like an extension of the alignment panel for the type tool.
- The next option in the Type Menu is **Anti-Alias**, this option is utilized to make the letter edges appear smooth. The majority of the letters will "appear blocky" and "hard-edged" if this option is not selected.
- The text can position itself "horizontally" and "vertically" with the following option, **Orientation**.
- **Create Work Path** converts texts to a path, **Convert to Shape** changes a text to a shape, **Rasterize Type layer** converts a layer type to a raster image,
- **Convert to Point text** converts texts to character type
- **Warp Text** allows you to twist your texts into any form
- **Match Fonts** searches your desktop fonts library and creative cloud storage to show you type fonts that are similar to the one you have selected in a design.
- **Font preview** allows you to decide how your fonts will be displayed when you type text. You can discover the other features in the type menu by exploring them too.

Select: The Select menu in Photoshop contains options related to selections.

You can choose or deselect each layer and item on the canvas from this menu. With a few useful and pertinent tools, you can choose a previous option again and flip it.

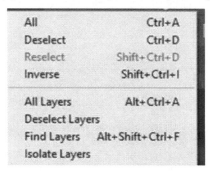

Advanced selection options like color range, focus area, subject, and sky are accessible in the select menu

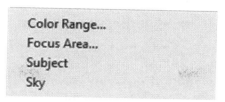

You can change the edge of a selection by using the **Refine Edge** tool in the **Select and Mask** tool, which is located in the Select menu. The smooth, feather, contrast, and shift edge parameters can be changed to define specific selection features.

You can adjust the size of your selection by using **Modify**. **Grow** automatically extends a selection to neighboring pixels in order to effectively increase the selection area. If you keep clicking it, more alternatives will show up.

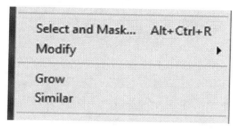

To re-select something later, use Save Selection and Load Selection. When you need to apply a new selection again, you can save it and then load it.

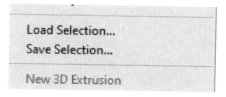

Filter: Adobe Photoshop filters are available under the Filter menu. To see a preview of the integrated artistic, brushstroke, distort, sketch, and texture filters, navigate to the **Filter Gallery** from this page.

Convert for Smart Filters allows you to convert an image or element into a smart object before applying your filter effects.

You can also access the **Neutral Filters, 3D, Adaptive Wide Angle, Camera Raw Filter, lens correction, Liquify**, and **Vanishing Point**.

31

Additionally, there are filters for blur, noise, pixelate, render, and sharpen in this menu. Go to **Filter** > **Other** > **Custom** and click the Load button to find an existing ACF file, or the Save button to create a new ACF file, to save or load a customized Photoshop filter.

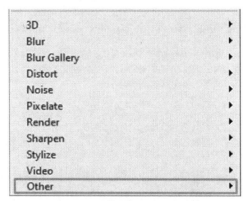

Using the Filter option, you can also offset vertically and horizontally to make it look like an image has been doubled over.

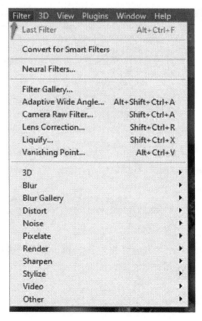

View: You may use the View option in Photoshop to modify how you see things. A ruler may be activated, full-screen mode can be selected, and guidelines can be made for precise placement.

Under Photoshop, zooming settings are located under the View menu. These choices include zooming in and out, displaying the print size, displaying the actual pixel size, and automatically resizing the canvas to fit the screen. Other features that you can show or hide from the View menu include selection edges, Pattern Review, Print Size, Actual Size, Screen Mode, target paths, notes, layer edges, edit pins, guides, slices, mesh, pixel grid, and brush preview.

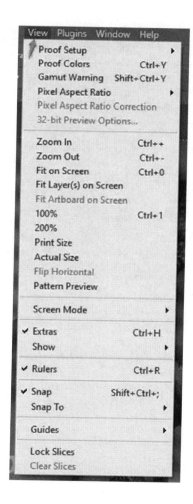

Plugins: You may directly access the plugins you have installed or want to install in your Photoshop software by selecting the plugins option in the menu bar. You are taken directly to the Plugins Panel after selecting the Plugins menu. Plugins can be downloaded, installed, and accessed from the Plugin panel at any time.

A plugin is a software add-on that is installed on a program, enhancing its capabilities.

Window: Photoshop's Window menu lets you customize your workspace by exposing and hiding windows. Accessible windows are not constantly visible, so utilize the Window menu to selectively expose or hide them as needed.

Use the Window menu to change whether a window is visible or hidden. Action, Tools, History, Layers, Notes, Paths, Adjustments, Brush, Channels, Color, History, and Channels are a few examples. Since you won't need them for your tasks all the time, it's a good idea to hide them to avoid cluttering your viewpoint.

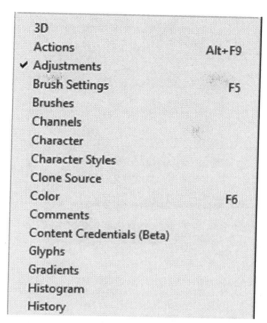

Use the **Arrange** and **Workspace** submenus to adjust the windows' positions. These menus do, however, have certain preset options for positioning windows in locations that are intended to make different tasks, like as painting and typography, easier. Additionally, you may drag and drop windows outside of Photoshop's main window and anywhere you choose.

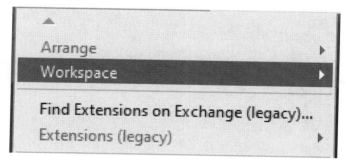

Help: The Help menu is the last item on Photoshop's menu bar. You may view the version of Photoshop you're using, see which plug-ins are presently loaded, register Photoshop with Adobe, access the Photoshop Support Centre, hands-on tutorials, the new features of Photoshop, and more.

The contents of your menu bar may be altered and shortcuts added, which is incredible. Use the steps shown below to change the items in your menu bar.

Use the steps below to add a panel to your workplace,

✦ Select **Windows** from the **Menu bar.**

✦ Select **Workspace** and click on **Keyboard Shortcuts and Menu**.

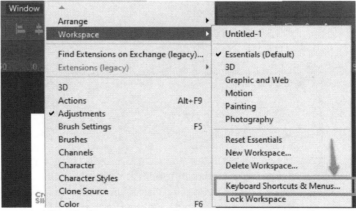

✦ At the upper side of the menu preview, select **Keyboard Shortcuts** to add shortcuts, and **Menus** to edit the contents of your menu.

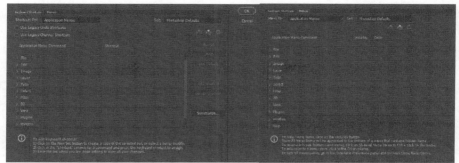

✦ Carefully study the Preview Menu to make edits to your satisfaction.

Photoshop's Tool Bar

The toolbar for Photoshop is on the screen's left side:

Usually, the toolbar is displayed as a single, long column. However, it can be reduced to a single, shorter column by clicking the two arrows at the top. Click the two arrows again to return to a one-column toolbar:

Let's take a look at Photoshop's toolbar structure. The tools are arranged systematically, with relevant objects grouped together, even though their display may appear to be random.

Every tool in the toolbar has an icon to represent it, and there are many more tools available than what we can see.

Additional tools are hidden beneath a tool icon in the same spot if it has a small arrow in the lower right corner.

To view the additional tools, click and hold the tool icon. Alternatively, you can right-click (Windows) or control-click (Mac) the icon. A fly-out menu listing the additional tools will show up.

The tool that is automatically displayed in each toolbar area is known as the default tool. However, the default tool isn't always visible in Photoshop. Instead, the last tool you select will be displayed.

The Move and **Selection tools** for Photoshop are located at the top. Additionally, the **Crop** and **Slice tools** are directly beneath them. The **Measurement tools** are listed next, then Photoshop's numerous **Retouching and Painting capabilities**.

The tools for **drawing** and **typing** come next. The **Navigation tools** are located at the bottom.

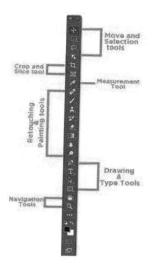

An Overview of Photoshop Tools

Note that, the bracketed letter at the front of each tool is the shortcut for the tools.

Move and Selection Tools

- **Move Tool (V):** Layers, selects, and guides can all be moved within a Photoshop document using the Move Tool. Enable "Auto-Select" so that the group or layer you click on is chosen automatically.

- **Artboard Tool (V):** The Artboard Tool makes it simple to build a range of web or UX (user experience) layouts for various devices or screen sizes.

- **Rectangular Marquee Tool (M):** Holding down Shift while dragging creates a square selection, and the Rectangular Marquee Tool creates rectangular selection outlines.

- **Elliptical Marquee Tool (M):** Elliptical Selections are outlined using the elliptical marquee tool, and you may hold down the Shift key to form a perfect circle selection.

- **Single Row Marquee Tool**: A single row of pixels in the image is selected from left to right using Photoshop's Single Row Marquee Tool.

- **Single Column Marquee Tool**: To choose a single column of pixels from top to bottom, use the Single Column Marquee Tool.

- **Lasso Tool (L):** You can create a freeform selection outline around an object using the Lasso Tool.

- **Polygonal lasso Tool (L):** To create a polygonal, straight-edged selection outline around an object, use the Polygonal Lasso Tool to click all around it.

- **Magnetic Lasso Tool (L):** When using the Magnetic Lasso Tool, the selection outline is fixed to the object's edges while your mouse cursor moves.

- **Object Selection Tool (L):** By just dragging a rough selection outline around an object, you can select it with the Object Selection Tool.

✦ **Quick Selection Tool (L):** You can quickly select an object using the Quick Selection Tool by simply painting a brush over it. For higher quality options, turn on "Auto-Enhance" in the Options Bar.

✦ **Magic Wand Tool (L):** With just one click, the Magic Wand Tool in Photoshop may select areas of similar color. The selection of colors depends on the "Tolerance" value in the Options Bar.

Crop and Slice Tools

✦ **Crop Tool (C):** When cropping an image in Photoshop, use the Crop Tool to eliminate any undesirable portions. To crop an image without destroying it, uncheck "Delete Cropped Pixels" in the Options Bar.

✦ **Perspective Crop Tool (C):** Use the Perspective Crop Tool to crop an image while also correcting common perspective or distortion issues.

✦ **Slice Tool (C):** The Slice Tool separates a layout or image into more manageable slices that may be exported and adjusted.

- **Slice Select Tool (C):** To select specific slices made with the Slice Tool, use the Slice Select Tool.

- **Frame Tool (K):** With the new Frame Tool in Photoshop CC 2019, you can insert photos into rectangular or elliptical forms, more like clipping the masks of the photo.

Measurement Tools

- **Eyedropper Tool (I):** Photoshop's Eyedropper Tool extracts color samples from a picture. Increase "Sample Size" in the Options Bar to see a clearer image of the color of the sampled area.

- **3D Material Eyedropper Tool (I):** To sample material from a 3D model in Photoshop, use the 3D Material Eyedropper Tool.

- **Color Sampler Tool (I):** The Colour Sampler Tool displays the color values for the selected (sampling) region of an image. It is possible to test up to four sites at once. Examine the color data in Photoshop's Info panel.

- **Ruler Tool (I):** The Ruler Tool calculates angles, distances, and positions. Perfect for placing graphics and other items precisely where you want them.

♦ **Note Tool (I):** Using the Note Tool, you can add text-based notes to your Photoshop document for your use or the use of other people involved in the same project. The PSD file's notes are also retained.

♦ **Count Tool:** Use Photoshop's Count Tool to manually count the objects in an image or to have it count multiple selected areas for you.

Retouching and Painting Tools

♦ **Spot Healing Brush Tool (J):** Photoshop's Spot Healing Brush can be used quickly to repair blemishes and other minor problems in an image. Select a brush size that is slightly larger than the spot for best results.

♦ **Healing Brush Tool (J):** To address larger problem locations in an image, use the Healing Brush by clicking while holding down Alt (Windows) or Option (Mac), then painting over the troubled area to sample a nice texture.

♦ **Patch Tool:** Create a freeform selection outline around a troublesome area using the Patch Tool. Drag the selection's outline over a region with good texture to fix it later.

- **Content-Aware Move Tool (J):** To select and move a specific section of an image, use the Content-Aware Move Tool. Photoshop uses components from the surrounding areas to automatically fill in the hole left by the original object.

- **Red Eye Tool (J):** The Red Eye Tool eliminates typical red eye issues in a photo brought on by camera flash.

- **Brush Tool (B):** The main painting tool in Photoshop is the Brush Tool. Apply it to a layer or layer mask to add brush strokes.

- **Pencil Tool:** Another painting tool in Photoshop is the Pencil Tool. However, whereas the Pencil Tool always paints with harsh edges, the Brush Tool can paint with soft-edged brush strokes.

- **Color Replacement Tool (B):** To quickly change an object's color to another, use Photoshop's Color Replacement Tool.

- **Mixer Brush Tool (B):** In contrast to the standard Brush Tool, Photoshop's Mixer Brush can mimic aspects of real painting, including color blending and combination as well as paint wetness.

- **Clone Stamp Tool (S):** The most fundamental retouching tool in Photoshop is the Clone Stamp Tool. To cover pixels in another area of the image, it samples pixels from one area of the image.

- **Pattern Stamp Tool (S):** To add a pattern to the image, use the Pattern Stamp Tool.

- **History Brush Tool (Y):** The History Brush Tool adds a snapshot from a previous stage (history state) to the image while it is currently being created. From the History panel, select the previous state.

- **Art History Brush Tool (Y):** Additionally, the Art History Brush adds a stylized snapshot of an earlier historical period to the image.

- **Eraser Tool (E):** Pixels on a layer are permanently erased by Photoshop's Eraser Tool. It can also be used to paint scenes from the past.

- **Background Eraser Tool (E):** By painting over them, the Background Eraser Tool removes similar-colored sections from an image.

✦ **Magic Eraser Tool (E):** In that, it picks regions of similar hue with a single click, the Magic Eraser Tool is comparable to the Magic Wand Tool. The Magic Eraser Tool, however, afterward permanently erases those regions.

✦ **Gradient Tool(G):** The Gradient Tool in Photoshop creates gradual color blending between various hues. You can design and create your gradients using the Gradient Editor.

✦ **Paint Bucket Tool (G):** The Paint Bucket Tool applies your Foreground color or a pattern to a region of similar color. The range of colors that will be impacted in the vicinity of the clicked area depends on the "Tolerance" value.

✦ **3D Material Drop Tool (G):** The 3D Material Drop Tool is used in 3D modeling and enables you to sample material from one part of your model, mesh, or 3D layer, then drop it into a different location.

✦ **Blur Tool:** When you use the tool to paint over an area, it blurs and softens it.

✦ **Sharpen Tool:** When you paint over an area, the Sharpen Tool sharpens it.

➕ **Smudge Tool:** The areas you paint over are smeared and smudged by Photoshop's Smudge Tool. It can also be applied to produce the appearance of finger painting.

➕ **Dodge Tool (O):** Use the Dodge Tool to paint over dark areas of the image to make them lighter.

➕ **Burn Tool (O):** The areas you paint over with the Burn Tool will become darker.

➕ **Sponge Tool (O):** Use the Sponge Tool to apply paint over specific areas to alter the color saturation.

Drawing and Type Tools

➕ **Pen Tools (P):** You may create incredibly accurate pathways, vector forms, or selections using Photoshop's Pen Tool.

➕ **Freeform Pen Tool (P):** Draw freehand paths or shapes using the Freeform Pen Tool. As you draw the path, anchor points are automatically added.

✦ **Curvature Pen Tool (P):** The Pen Tool has been streamlined and made easier with the Curvature Pen Tool. Since Photoshop CC 2018.

✦ **Add Anchor Point Tool:** To add more anchor points along a path, use the Add Anchor Point Tool.

✦ **Delete Anchor Point Tool:** Using the Delete Anchor Point Tool, click on an existing anchor point along a path to eliminate it.

✦ **Convert Point Tool:** Using the Convert Point Tool, click on a path's smooth anchor point to change it into a corner point. To change a corner point into a smooth point, click on it.

✦ **Horizontal Type Tool (T):** Use the Horizontal Type Tool, also known as the Type Tool in Photoshop, to add conventional type to your document.

✦ **Vertical Type Tool:** The Vertical Type Tool adds type vertically from top to bottom.

- **Vertical Type Mask Tool (T):** The Vertical Type Mask Tool makes an editable selection outline in the form of vertical type, as opposed to adding editable text to your project.

- **Horizontal Type Mask Tool (T):** The Horizontal Type Mask Tool produces a selection outline that resembles type, just like the Vertical Mask Type Tool does. The type is added horizontally as opposed to vertically, though.

- **Path Selection Tool (A):** To select and move an entire path at once in Photoshop, use the Path Selection Tool (the black arrow).

- **Direct Selection Tool (A):** An individual path segment, anchor point, or direction handle can be selected and moved using the Direct Selection Tool (the white arrow).

- **Rectangle Tool (U):** With sharp or rounded corners, the Rectangle Tool creates rectangular vector shapes, paths, or pixel shapes. To force the shape into a perfect square, drag while holding down Shift.

- **Eclipse Tool (U):** Drawing elliptical vector, path, or pixel forms is possible with the Ellipse Tool. To draw a complete circle, hold down Shift while dragging.

- **Triangle Tool (U):** Triangle shapes are created by the Triangle Tool. To draw an equilateral triangle, hold down Shift. To round the corners, select the Radius option.

- **Polygon Tool (U):** The polygon tool can draw any number of sides as polygonal shapes. To transform polygons into stars, select the Star Ratio option.

- **Line Tool (U):** The Line Tool can draw arrows or straight lines. To alter the line's appearance, change the stroke's weight and color.

- **Custom Shape Tool (U):** You can choose and create custom shapes using Photoshop's Custom Shape Tool. Choose from hundreds of pre-built custom shapes in Photoshop or make your own.

Navigation Tools

- **Hand Tool (H):** When an image is zoomed in, we can move it around the screen by clicking and dragging it.

- **Rotate View Tool (R):** To view and edit the image from various perspectives, rotate the canvas using Photoshop's Rotate View Tool.

- **Zoom Tool (Z):** To focus on a particular area of the image, use the Zoom Tool to click on the image. Click with the Zoom Tool while holding down Alt (Windows) or Option (Mac) to zoom out.

To add shortcuts to your tools, do the following.

- Select **Windows** from the **Menu bar.**

- Select **Workspace** and click on **Keyboard Shortcuts and Menu**.

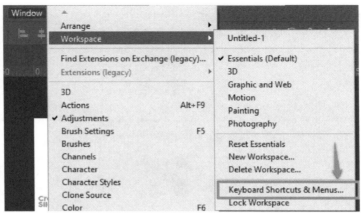

* At the upper side of the menu preview, select **Keyboard Shortcuts** to add shortcuts, click on **Shortcut For** and select **Tools.**

* Click on the current shortcut commands and change it to the command of your choice.

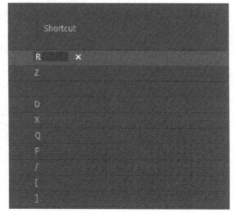

Managing Windows and Panels
Do the following to hide/display all tabs.

- Press the **Tab** key on your keyboard to see or conceal all panels, including the Tools and Control panels.
- Press **Shift + Tab** to see or hide all panels besides the Tools and Control panels.

One or two columns can be used to display the tools in the Tools panel at the same time. To accomplish this, adhere to the guidelines provided below.

- Click the double arrow at the top of the Tool Panel

Your files/projects are presented in tabs when you open more than one file in Photoshop.

You can arrange your tabs in different ways by following the instructions below.

- Select **Windows** on the **Menu Bar**

- After selecting **Arrange**, click on any tab options of your choice that suit the project you're working on. You can also try out all the options to find the one that best suits you.

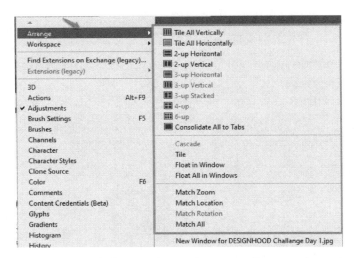

You can group your panels into docks to arrange them. A collection of panels is called a dock. Panels can be moved to the workspace's edge to form a dock by creating a drop zone. When a dock's panels are removed, the dock vanishes.

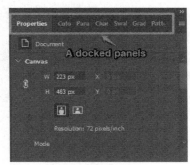

Do the following to dock or undock panels.

- Drag the panel by its title bar into a dock (a group of panels).
- Drag the panel by its title bar to undock.
- To remove a panel and put it into another dock, drag the panel from the original and insert it into the new dock.

A panel can float freely if it is dragged out of its dock without being placed in another. You can place the floating panel anywhere in the workplace. Panel groups or floating panels can be stacked such that when you slide the topmost title bar, they move together.

To collapse and expand a panel, do the following.

✦ Click on the double arrow at the top of the dock.

CHAPTER THREE

BASIC CONCEPTS & PRACTICAL TUTORIALS IN PHOTOSHOP

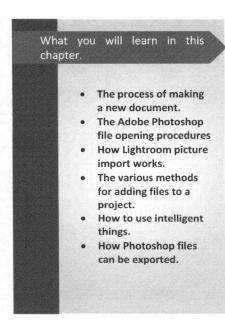

What you will learn in this chapter.

- **The process of making a new document.**
- **The Adobe Photoshop file opening procedures**
- **How Lightroom picture import works.**
- **The various methods for adding files to a project.**
- **How to use intelligent things.**
- **How Photoshop files can be exported.**

Working with Documents/Projects

You are already familiar with Photoshop, so you should know that starting a new document in Photoshop is as important as starting the artwork. In this section, we'll look at "How to Create a New Document in Photoshop".

Creating A New Document

In Photoshop, you can create a new document by choosing one of the options. Follow these procedures to create a new document:

✦ **Launch Photoshop**: Your Home Screen will be open if you are using Photoshop CC. This display is continuously changing.

✦ Press Ctrl + N (Cmd + N) or select **File** > **New**.

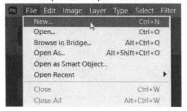

✦ The New Document dialog box appears in either case.

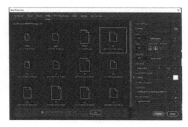

✦ Before starting a new document, make changes to the preset on the right panel. There are various choices available to you:

56

- o "Photo," "Print," "Art & Illustration," "Web," "Mobile," and "Film & Video" are the **preset options**.
- o **Name**: Enter a file name for the new document.
- o **Width & Height**: Indicate the New Document's size. Select the unit from the pop-up menu as well.
- o **Orientation**: Landscape or portrait is the preferred page orientation for the New Document.
- o **Artboards**: Choosing this option while creating a new document adds an artboard. It could be added later as well.
- o Selecting **Color Mode & Bit** for the New Document. You will primarily employ CMKY (for print purposes), RGB (for digital purposes), and Grayscale (for Black and White) (rarely) in 8-bit out of the five available color modes.
- o **Resolution**: The quality of an image is determined by its resolution. You should use 72 PPI for digital purposes (pixel-per-inch). Ideally, you should choose 300 PPI for printing (industrial standard resolution).
- o **Background Content**: You can select a different color from the options even though White is the default setting for a New Document.
- ✦ Click Advanced Choices to specify the additional options.

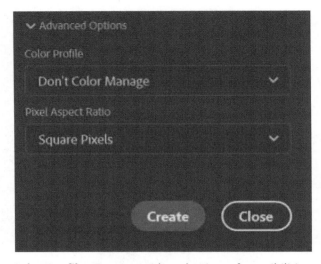

- o **Color Profile**: From a wide selection of possibilities, select the color profile for your New Document.
- o **Pixel Aspect Ratio**: The proportion of a pixel's width to height.
- ✤ After configuring all the options, click the "**Create**" button to start a new document.

There are multiple methods for adding a picture to Photoshop. Whether you utilize **Commands, drag and drop**, or **import from a desktop file manager or picture database like Lightroom**, your photos will always be imported in the highest quality. However, as this does not ensure exceptionally sharp images, there are alternative methods to verify the image data already during the import. In this section, you will discover Photoshop's import options and how to use them in your workflow.

Files can be opened using the **Open** and **Open Recent** commands. Additionally, files from other Adobe applications, such as Bridge, Fresco, Lightroom, and Illustrator, can be imported into Photoshop.

You must first enter settings and parameters in a dialogue window before you can fully open some files in Photoshop, like Camera Raw and PDF.

In addition to still photos, users who use Photoshop may open and edit, movies, and picture sequence files.

A wide range of file formats can be imported and opened in Photoshop using the Plug-in modules. If a file format is absent from the Open dialogue box or the **File > Import** submenu, you may need to install the plug-in module for that format.

Do the following to open a file using the **Open Command**.

✦ Choose **File > Open**.

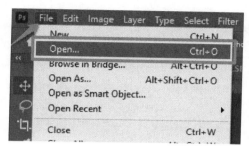

✦ Choose the file name you want to open. Choose the option to display all files from the Files of Type (Windows) or Enable (Mac OS) pop-up menu if the file is missing.

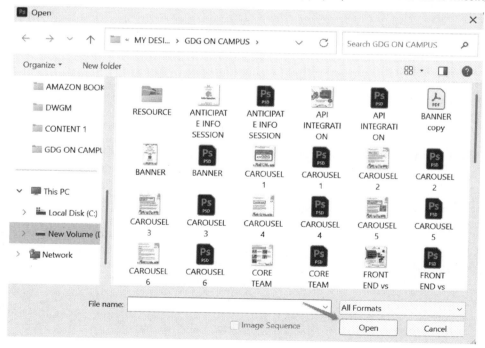

✦ Click **Open**. In some circumstances, a dialog window that lets you configure options specific to the format appears.

Using The Open Recent Command
✦ Select a file from the submenu by selecting **File** > **Open Recent**.

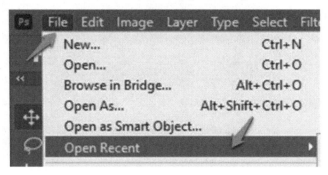

Inserting Images Via Drag & Drop
Often, the drag-and-drop method is one of the simplest ways to load photos into Photoshop.

✦ Open Photoshop and drag a photo from Explorer or your desktop onto the Photoshop user interface.
✦ Release the left mouse button to create a new document

The image's resolution, width, length, and color mode are all precisely the same in the enclosed document as they were in the original.

Importing Images from Lightroom
In addition to importing your photos, Lightroom lets you review and arrange them. You can arrange your photos using Adobe Cloud Storage instead of storing them on your computer.

- Click the (**+**) symbol in the upper left corner of Photoshop after opening your Photoshop.
- Next, select the picture you want to import into Explorer and press "**Review For Import**."
- To upload the picture to Adobe Cloud, click Add Photos in the upper right corner. A small cloud emblem with a spinning blue progress wheel will then appear in the upper right corner. After a short while, this icon disappeared, indicating that your photo has now been uploaded to the cloud and is ready to be imported into Photoshop.

To *import* images from Lightroom, do the following,

- Launch Photoshop and select the Start workspace's **Lr Photos tab**, there is a list of the pictures that have already been added.
- To access the most recent version of your image database, including the most recent photo you uploaded, click the **Refresh** button.
- Now select **Import Selected** after clicking this picture. The image is then downloaded to your local computer where it can be edited as usual.

Inserting Images/Files in existing documents

As in the first example, you can import an image by simply dragging and dropping it into an existing document. If the newly imported image is not displayed throughout the document's width and height after import, it can be too small to be scaled to the document's size (see image). This allows the picture to be inserted into an already-existing document in its best possible quality. In this case, Photoshop's Smart Objects tool is helpful. After a photo is imported into an existing document, Photoshop turns it into a smart object. A reminder of this is provided by the small file icon in the thumbnail's right-hand corner. Double-clicking the thumbnail will open the newly imported photo as a separate but connected document.

Inserting Files via Place Embedded

When working on individual photographs, it's acceptable to have separate documents open without requiring them to interact with one another. Therefore, in some situations, open command is excellent.

However, what if we desired to combine or blend the two pictures? Therefore, it is pointless to have them in different documents. Rather, we require a method for opening both images into a single document. Thus, image placement is crucial. Use Photoshop's Place Embedded function to add a picture.

- ⬍ In the **File Menu** drop-down, Select **Place Embedded**

✦ Then go to the folder on your PC where your photographs are stored. Select the portrait image by clicking on it, then click **Place**.

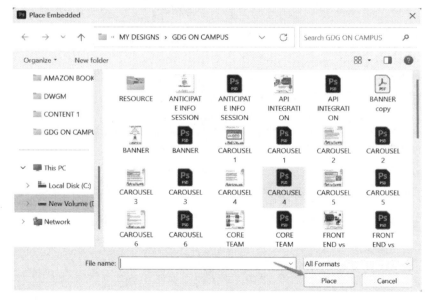

Inserting files via Place-linked

When working on individual photographs, it's acceptable to have separate documents open without requiring them to interact with one another. Therefore, in some situations, open command is excellent.

However, what if we desired to combine or blend the two pictures? Therefore, it is pointless to have them in different documents. Rather, we require a method for opening both images into a single document. Thus, image placement is crucial. Use Photoshop's Place Embedded function to add a picture.

Follow these steps to Place Linked:

- In the **File** menu drop-down, select **placed linked**

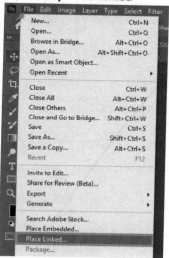

- Select an appropriate file and click **Place**.

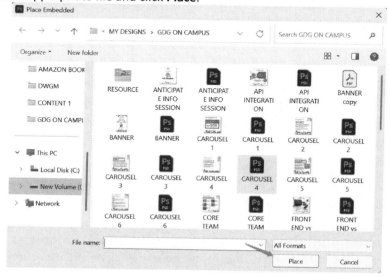

The Linked Smart Object is created and is displayed in the **Layers** panel with a link icon (⬛).

The associated Linked Smart Object is automatically updated whenever a Photoshop document that refers to an external source file is opened and that file changes. However, when you open a Photoshop project with out-of-synch Linked Smart Objects, you can update the Smart Objects:

✦ Right-click a Linked Smart Object layer and choose **Update Modified Content**.
✦ Choose **Layer** > **Smart Objects** > **Update Modified Content**

The Layers panel visibly indicates Linked Smart Objects whose Source Images have changed:

✦ Out-of-sync Linked Smart Objects are highlighted in the Layers panel.

✦ Linked Smart Objects with missing external source files are highlighted in the Layers panel.

The actions below should be followed to resolve a Linked Smart Object with a missing external source:

✦ **Resolve Broken Link** can be selected by right-clicking on the Linked Smart Object layer icon.
✦ Navigate to the missing object's new location.
✦ Toggle **Place**.

You can save the Linked Smart Objects source files to a folder on your computer by packaging them in a Photoshop document. The folder contains a copy of the Photoshop document and the source files.

✦ Choose **File** > **Package**.
✦ Select a location where you want to place the source files and a copy of the Photoshop document.

Any audio or video Linked Smart Objects in the document are packaged as well.

Place Embedded vs Place Linked
Unlike linked smart objects, embedded smart objects are not connected to the source image once they are in Photoshop. Since the source picture is linked to a linked smart

64

object, the linked smart object will likewise be deleted if the source image is deleted. Put differently, it breaks.

.

- ✦ Photoshop creates a huge file when a media file is embedded because it adds the original size of the smart object to the size of the image to which it is added. However, because a linked smart object is connected to an external picture source, it only significantly enlarges the image to which it is added.
- ✦ An embedded smart object does not experience this since its totality is already in the current file, while a linked smart object becomes damaged or flawed if its source image is removed.
  A connected smart object must be updated using **Update Modified Content**, whereas an embedded smart object is updated automatically if its source picture is altered and saved elsewhere.
- ✦ An embedded smart object can be linked by clicking on **relink to file.**
- ✦ Using **Place Embedded** is best when you're working alone while **Place Linked** is better when you are working with a large team.
- ✦ A PSD containing a linked smart object is best transported through the **package** option.

It is possible to transform an embedded Smart Object into a connected Smart Object. The filters of the embedded Smart Object change, while other effects remain intact.

Do the following:

- ✦ In the Photoshop document, choose a **Smart Object** layer that is embedded.
- ✦ Select **Layer > Smart Object > Convert To Linked** from the menu.
- ✦ Choose the computer's location where you wish to save the source file. Give the file a name and an extension that is supported. For illustration, link file.jpg

Do the following to filter your layer panel with smart objects.

- ✦ Choose **Smart Object** from the filtering pop-up menu in the Layers panel.

✤ Click one of the following icons:

    o   Filter for up-to-date Linked Smart Objects

    o   Filter for out-of-synch Linked Smart Objects

    o   Filter for missing Linked Smart Objects

    o   Filter for embedded Smart Objects

The layers of an embedded or connected smart object can be separated out and then instantly integrated into a Photoshop project. The extra layers are unpacked into a new layer group in the Layers panel if the Smart Object contains more than one layer. Transforms and Smart Filters on multi-layered Smart Objects are lost upon unpacking.

✤ From the Layers panel, pick the **Smart Object layer**.
✤ Attempt one of the following:
    o   Click the Smart Object layer with the right mouse button (Windows) or control button (Mac) and choose **Convert To Layers** from the context menu.
    o   Select **Layer** > **Smart Objects** > **Convert To Layers** from the menu bar.
    o   Click **Convert To Layers** in the **Properties panel**.
    o   Select **Convert To Layers** from the **Options menu** of the Layers panel.
    o   In the Layers panel, the layers are unpacked into a layer group.

You can rasterize a Smart Object's contents to a regular layer if you are done editing the Smart Object data. The transforms, warps, and filters that have been applied to a Smart Object are no longer editable once it has been rasterized.

✦ Select the Smart Object, and choose **Layer** > **Smart Objects** > **Rasterize**.

Do the following to convert the contents of a smart object.

✦ Choose **Layer** > **Smart Objects** > **Export Contents** after selecting the Smart Object from the Layers menu.
✦ Click **Save** after deciding where to save the Smart Object's data.

Photoshop exports the Smart Object in its selected format, which may be JPEG, AI, TIF, PDF, or another format. If the Smart Object was constructed using layers, it is exported in PSB format.

Working with Smart objects
In Photoshop or Illustrator files, for example, layers containing picture data from raster or vector pictures are referred to as "Smart Objects." Because Smart Objects preserve the original characteristics of an image's underlying material, you can alter the layer without causing any harm.

It is possible to embed an image's contents inside a Photoshop document. Photoshop allows you to create Linked Smart Objects with content that references external image files. The contents of a Linked Smart Object are updated whenever a source image file changes.

Duplicated instances of a Smart Object are not the same as linked Smart Objects in a Photoshop document. Using a shared source file across many Photoshop works is a well-known and appreciated concept for web designers: linked smart objects.

Benefits of Smart Objects

Smart Objects allow you to:

✦ Make non-destructive adjustments. Since the transformations do not affect the real image data, you can warp, rotate, skew, distort, scale or perspective transform a layer without sacrificing quality or information.
✦ Work with vector data, such as Illustrator's vector art, that Photoshop frequently rasterizes.
✦ You should use nondestructive filtering. Filters for Smart Objects can be modified at any time.
✦ Any instance of a Smart Object that is edited will be immediately updated. Before application, link or unlink a layer mask to the Smart Object layer.
✦ Try out various layouts with low-resolution placeholder photos that you will eventually swap out for the final goods.

It's important to understand that a Smart Object layer cannot be directly subjected to painting, dodging, burning, or cloning operations; instead, it must first be converted into a regular layer before being rasterized. To perform operations that alter the pixel data, you can update copies of the Smart Object, clone a new layer above the Smart Object layer, edit the contents of a Smart Object, or create a new layer.

Placed Embedded and **Placed Linked** are the two major ways to insert a smart object into a document in Photoshop.

Exporting Files out of Photoshop

When working with photographs in Photoshop, you may save your work in three different ways: **Save**, **Save As**, and **Export**. A duplicate of your image will be preserved by each of these choices, but there are some key differences between them.

Save is the primary way to store your work in Photoshop. You can save your project as a PSD file and save changes using this operation.

To use **Save**, do the following.

✦ Select **File** from the **Menu Bar** and click on **Save**.

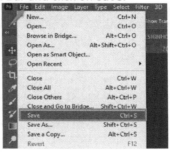

You can create a new copy of your image with a different file name by choosing **Save As**. This is useful if you want to save your work in many file formats or create multiple copies of an image.

To use **Save As**, follow the procedure below

✦ When you are ready to export your file, simply Select **Save A**s from the **File** menu drop-down.

68

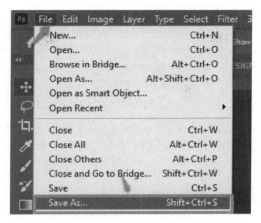

* Select your storage, either **save on your computer** or **save to Creative Cloud**.

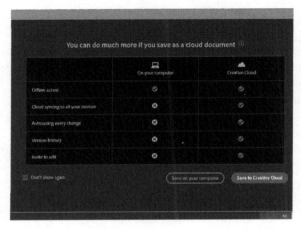

* Either of the options you choose, the next preview box allows you to select the file format you desire to save your document in, then select **save**

Export is the backup way to save your work in Photoshop. A new version of your image is created using the same information when you select Export.

The following are the formats you can save your files in.

* **Photoshop Document (PSD):** Of all the file formats that Photoshop accepts, the PSD format is probably the most important. "Photoshop Document," or PSD, is the default file type in Photoshop. PSD is one of the few file formats that can completely support Photoshop's powerful features, including layers, layer masks, adjustment layers, channels, paths, and more. It also functions as your working file.

When we view a picture in Photoshop, it temporarily converts it into a PSD file so we may use all of Photoshop's tools, commands, and features, regardless of the original file type. The sole real disadvantage of PSD files is that they can get very large, particularly when working on images with hundreds or even thousands of layers. Your PSD file is the most important thing you may have, therefore save a master copy of your work as one so you can access it in Photoshop whenever you need to.

- **Joint Picture Experts Group (JPG or JPEG):** This format is perfect for images with a lot of color, such as continuous tone images and photographs. JPEG may achieve excellent compression ratios while maintaining crystal-clear image quality.

- **Graphical Interchange Format (GIF):** The standard file format for web graphics is GIF (Graphics Interchange Format), which is even older than JPEG. "web graphics," I said, not "web photos." GIF files can only display 256 colors, which is significantly less than the hundreds of colors needed to properly replicate a photograph (and even fewer than the millions of colors that the JPEG format supports). However, for online design, the GIF format is essential. When the files contain a lot of solid colors, they perform especially well for buttons, banners, and web page layouts. All of the major online browsers accept GIF files, and they load quickly due to their small file sizes.

- **Portable Network Graphics (PNG):** PNG (Portable Network Graphics) was developed as an alternative to GIF (also known as "PNG not GIF"). Even if it never happened and GIF files are still commonly used today, the PNG format performs better than the GIF format in practically every way. It even improves the JPEG format. JPEG files only offer 24-bit color (16.7 million colors), whereas PNG files allow up to 48-bit color, which gives us over 1 billion possible colors. This format is a lossless storage format that uses patterns in the image to compress the image. The uncompressed version of the image is comparable to the original because PNG less compression is completely reversible. PNG is a superb choice for maintaining high-quality digital photos as originals. The disadvantage is that PNG is not as widely accepted as JPEG and does not support CMYK color, which makes it unusable by professional printers. For daily viewing and sharing of your digital images, the JPEG format is still more convenient and practical, despite the fact that the image quality isn't as great.

- **TIFF (Tagged Image File Format):** Because TIFF (Tagged Image File Format) provides lossless compression, you may retain images with the highest quality possible, making it another great choice for image archiving. Similar to PSD files, TIFF files are among the few file formats that can utilize every function of Photoshop. The quality comes at a price because TIFF files can be somewhat large, especially when compared to JPEG files. TIFF is the most popular format for photos meant for commercial printing, and it works with practically every page layout program, such as QuarkXPress and InDesign. This format is particularly flexible because it can be based on either a lossy or lossless compression algorithm. Details regarding the compression technique are included in the image itself. TIFF files are very large since they usually use a lossless picture storage method.

✥ **Encapsulated PostScript (EPS):** EPS (Encapsulated PostScript) is another well-known print industry standard format, however its use has been declining over time. EPS files are not picture files in the traditional sense. Rather, they provide instructions on how to print the image on a printer. Although the files are practically locked and cannot be altered until they are reopened in Photoshop, they can still be imported into the majority of page layout applications due to the "encapsulated" element. It is unlikely that you will use it frequently unless your commercial printer specifically asks for it.

✥ **Portable Document Format (PDF):** Although most people are already familiar with utilizing PDF files for viewing, sharing, and printing electronic documents (hence the name), the Portable Document Format (PDF) is becoming a popular choice for storing photos that are meant to be printed. All of Photoshop's features, including the use of spot colors, are supported and preserved in the PDF format, whereas the EPS format does not. The PSD and TIFF formats function similarly. In PDFs, you have the option of JPEG or lossless ZIP compression. You can balance image quality and file size with JPEG's Quality setting. Anyone with the free Adobe Reader program installed on their computer can read the image in PDF format.

To use **Export**, follow the procedure below,

✥ Select **Export** from the **File** menu drop-down

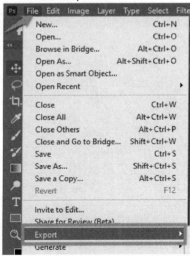

✦ Select how you want to export your work in the next drop-down menu

Quick Export as PNG	
Export As...	Alt+Shift+Ctrl+W
Export Preferences...	
Save for Web (Legacy)...	Alt+Shift+Ctrl+S
Artboards to Files...	
Artboards to PDF...	
Export For Aero...	
Layer Comps to Files...	
Layer Comps to PDF...	
Layers to Files...	
Color Lookup Tables...	
Data Sets as Files...	
Paths to Illustrator...	
Render Video...	

✦ You can explore the options and pick the one that suits your desire.

CHAPTER FOUR

DIGITAL IMAGES AND COLOR MODES IN PHOTOSHOP

What you will learn in this chapter.

- **Definition of digital images.**
- **Definition of image resolutions.**
- **The various Photoshop color modes and how to use them efficiently.**

Understanding Digital Images

Picture components, often known as pixels, make up a computer image. "Picture element" is abbreviated as "pixel," since pixels are the unimportant building blocks of all digital images. Just like a painting is made up of individual brushstrokes, a digital image is made up of individual pixels. When looking at a photo at a normal zoom level (100 percent or less) in Photoshop, the pixels are usually too small to notice. Rather, what we see seems to be a single image, with light, shadows, colors, and textures all working together to create a scene that is very similar to what would be seen in the real world.

Digital images can be divided into two groups based on how they are stored: **Raster/Bitmap** images and **Vector** images. Knowing the characteristics of each format can assist you in selecting the best one for your project because each has benefits and drawbacks that are pertinent to specific circumstances.

- ⬦ **Vector Image:** Mathematical lines and curves are used to store vector images. Vectors are used to hold information like as thickness, color, and length. Any output, size, and resolution can be used to display these images. Regretfully, Photoshop is raster-based and creates images using pixels. Photoshop was created especially for editing and creating raster-based images. Originally designed for photographers, the application has now grown to assist a variety of artists in creating a vast array of work. The nature of raster images in Photoshop will be covered in detail in the future section, but for now, let's look at vector images. Vector files are the ideal choice when a design needs to be scalable since they retain crisp detail at any scale. The vector format is a fantastic choice for digital pictures such as logos. If a vector file is converted to a raster file, the advantages of the vector format will be gone forever. The common vector file extensions are SVG, EPS, and EMF.
- ⬦ **Raster/Bitmap Images**: The ideal format for storing and displaying high-quality photos is raster files, often known as bitmaps. Most photographs are in the raster file format, whether they are digital or printed.

Using programs like Adobe Photoshop, you can change individual pixels in a raster file to change how a photograph looks. A bitmap or raster image is a rectangular array of sampled data or pixels. These images have a fixed number of pixels. When zooming in on a raster image, mathematical interpolation is employed; after a particular zooming factor value, the quality of the zoomed-in image decreases. The resolution of a bitmap image is determined by the sensing device. BMP, GIF, PNG, TIFF, and JPEG are examples of common bitmap or raster image formats.

.

Practical Applications
You can see pixels in Photoshop by using the Pixel Grid. Follow the instructions below to enable and disable the pixel grid.

- Select the **View Menu** in the **Menu Bar**,
- Select **Show**, and then choose Pixel Grid- To turn it back on, just select it again

Image resolution is another real-world use for pixels in Photoshop. The number of pixels in an image, measured vertically from top to bottom and horizontally from left to right, is known as image resolution. Image resolution controls how big or small photographs print and look on the screen based on the current picture size. The amount of visual detail expressed in pixel dimensions, such as 640 by 480 pixels, the horizontal dimension before the vertical, can also be referred to as digital picture resolution. The standard unit of measurement for image resolution is PPI, or "pixels per inch." More pixels per inch (PPI) at higher resolutions translate into more pixel information and a sharper, higher-quality image.

Lower-resolution images include fewer pixels, and if those pixels are too huge (typically occurs when an image is stretched), they may become extremely hazy and ambiguous. The size of a picture depends on how many pixels are packed into each inch of paper, both horizontally and vertically. This is why "PPI," or pixels per inch, is used to denote the resolution value. The more pixels we squeeze together on the page, the smaller the image will print because there are only so many pixels in the image.

.

Understanding Color Modes

The way the components of a color are blended depends on the number of color channels in a color mode. Differentiating the color modes is crucial for designers to maximize each step of the creative process. Choosing the appropriate color scheme for your design can also aid in communicating your tone and message. In this session, we'll identify the common color modes and discuss when to apply them in your designs.

CMYK, RGB, Bitmap, Greyscale, Indexed, Duotone, Lab, and Multichannel color modes are all supported by Photoshop Elements. The context in which your user uses a design dictates the color mode to utilize. Every color mode has a certain goal in mind.

RGB Color Mode

Red, green, and blue are the colors used in Photoshop RGB Color mode to create a variety of color options. Only digital formats, such as those on computer monitors, mobile devices, and television screens, support the RGB color mode. Despite being a common color scheme, the precise color spectrum that RGB represents might change based on the display device or application.

Depending on the working space setting you select in the Color Settings dialogue box, Photoshop's RGB Color mode changes. Instead of using ink to create hues, the RGB profile creates color by combining light in an additive manner. When all RGB colors are present and at their highest intensity, white is produced; when all colors are absent, black is produced. As a result, your device's screen appears black when you turn it off because it lacks RGB color. The color displays on your screen are caused by these RGB fundamental colors.

RGB is best used for digital designs alone. Set your documents to RGB for creating content for digital design, social media, websites, apps, or online marketing. Any image you create for a computer screen should be in RGB. Even though CMYK can be used for digital design, its narrow color gamut will restrict the range of colors you can use.

CMYK Color Mode

A range of tones can be produced by combining the four colors that comprise the CMYK color mode: Cyan, Magenta, Yellow, and Key (Black). This four-color method works with most printer kinds. Printed graphics are just a set of four-color dots arranged in layers to create different gradations and colors. Dots per inch are produced when printing using the CMYK color profiles. Although CMYK is a widely used color model, the exact range of colors it represents might vary according to the press and printing conditions.

Cyan, magenta, yellow, and black are the four ink colors used in the Process color, which are produced as millions of tiny, overlapping dots that combine to provide the whole color spectrum.

For designs that will be printed, only use CMYK. Use CMYK when creating business cards, letterheads, posters, brochures, and packaging. Use CMYK mode rather than RGB when creating an image for process color printing since CMYK conversion results in color separation. It is advised to edit in RGB first if you start with an RGB image then switch to CMYK after you're done. For the sake of both you and the printer, please check the color mode again before exporting a document for printing. By doing this, the possibility of color imbalance while converting RGB colors into their CMYK counterparts will be eliminated.

LAB Color Mode

The LAB color mode, sometimes referred to as CIELab (pronounced See-Lab), is based on the human perception of color. There are two color channels (A and B) and one lightness channel (L) in the color mode. The range of the Lightness channel (L) is 0 to 100, but the range of the Green-Red Axis channel (A) and Blue-Yellow Axis channel (B) is +127 to -128. Three color characteristics—saturation, hue, and lightness—determine the Lab mode.

Because it ensures that the colors seem the same, LAB color would be a great choice for creating branded items like banners, coffee mugs, and t-shirts. Color management systems utilize LAB as a color reference to consistently change color from one color mode to another. Furthermore, LAB can be used to improve the images' color vibrancy and naturalness.

Indexed Color Mode

The Index color mode is used to create 8-bit picture files with a maximum color count of 256. This color mode is only supported by digital formats, like those on television displays, mobile devices, and computer monitors. Adobe claims that when an image is converted to index color, its colors are stored and indexed in a color table. If a color from the original image is not in the database, the software either chooses the closest color or uses a dithering effect to approximate the color.

Despite having a limited color palette, index color can minimize file size without sacrificing the visual quality needed for websites, mobile applications, and digital presentations. As a result, index color mode is ideal for image optimization. For extensive editing, you should briefly switch to RGB mode as this mode only permits a certain degree of manipulation.

It is a wonderful choice for creating websites, mobile applications, and digital presentations.

Grayscale Color Mode

Different shades of grey make up the Greyscale mode. 8-bit graphics can contain up to 256 different hues of grey. The brightness of each pixel in a greyscale image ranges from 0 (black) to 255 (white). Compared to 8-bit photographs, 16- and 32-bit images have a lot more tones. Grayscale should only be utilized for digital and print designs. Use greyscale in digital formats to express a specific tone in your designs. When printing, use greyscale to save money and use as little ink as feasible.

Another characteristic of Photoshop's greyscale color mode is that an image must be converted to it before it can access the bitmap, multichannel, and duotone color modes.

Bitmap Color Mode

In bitmap mode, an image's pixels are represented by one of two color values: black or white. Because bitmap pictures have a bit depth of 1, they are called bitmapped 1-bit images. The Bitmap mode, sometimes called line art, uses black and white pixels. There are no hues or shades of grey in bitmap graphics. Both print and digital media can use this method. In digital formats, black-and-white values represent the pixels of a picture. In print media, black ink dots and white paper depict the entire image.

A Bitmap Image

Only digital and print designs should employ bitmaps. Bitmaps can be used to mimic both hand-drawn sketches and line drawings. Additionally, it can be used to mimic the look of an old illustration. Although bitmap graphics may appear to have jagged edges when seen on a screen, they frequently print smoothly and cleanly when the print resolution is high enough.

In Photoshop, you must first switch your color mode from RGB or CMYK (depending on the color mode you're using) to greyscale before you can utilize the bitmap color mode on an image.

Duotone Color Mode

The duotone mode creates monochrome, duotone (two-color), tritone (three-color), and quadtone (four-color) greyscale images using one to four custom inks. Only when an image has been converted to greyscale color mode can it be used in duotone color mode. Using duotone effects on your website and in your work is a terrific approach to combine and strengthen your brand and its colors.

Multichannel Color Mode

Because each channel contains 256 grey levels, the multichannel color mode is helpful for specialty printing. Multichannel mode photos can be saved in the following formats: Photoshop, Photoshop Raw, Photoshop DCS 2.0, Photoshop 2.0, or Large Document Format (PSB).

When converting photos to Multichannel mode, keep in mind these rules:

- Layers lose support and become flattened.
- The converted image uses the color channels from the original image to create spot color channels.

- When a CMYK image is converted to Multichannel mode, cyan, magenta, yellow, and black spot channels are created.
- When an RGB image is transformed to Multichannel mode, cyan, magenta, and yellow spot channels are created.
- When a channel is removed from an RGB, CMYK, or Lab image, the image immediately transitions to Multichannel mode, flattening the layers.

Save a multichannel image in Photoshop DCS 2.0 format before exporting.

CHAPTER FIVE

LAYERS; ONE OF THE FINEST TOOLS IN PHOTOSHOP

Understanding Layers

Have you ever wondered how Photoshop produces such stunning effects? Professionals use Photoshop layers on nearly every job, even though there are alternative methods for altering photographs. Perhaps the most crucial thing you can do to advance your Photoshop abilities is to learn how to use layers. The goal of layers, the many kinds of layers, and the fundamentals of layer generation and use will all be covered in this lesson.

Layers in Photoshop are individual slices of information that can be stacked or rearranged to create the composition of your image. Layers in Photoshop allow you to work non-destructively by stacking images on top of other images without interacting and mixing the pixels of images. Multiple photos can be stacked, text can be added to an image, vector graphics can be added, etc. using layers.

Photoshop has many different layers, but they may be broadly categorized into three groups: **Adjustment**, **Content**, and **Empty Layers**.

* **Content Layers**: different forms of content, including images, text, and shapes, are contained within these levels.
    o **Background Layers**: The Background Layer is the layer that comes with a photo when you initially open it in Photoshop. Many filters and effects cannot be applied to the Background Layer because it is protected. All background layers are called "Background" and are locked or protected by default. Double-clicking the layer name in the Layers Palette to unprotect the background brings up a dialogue box where you can change the layer name and other information. Once you click OK, your layer will no longer be protected.

o **Image layer**: Image layers contain any information about the picture. By default, a new layer is always created as an Image Layer. The Layer Thumbnail of Image Layers provides an overview of the layer's contents.

o **Type Layer**: Type Layers only contain live type. They can be created and modified using the Type Tool.

o **Fill Layer**: Solid colors, gradients, and patterns can all be used as fill layers. By selecting **Layer > New Fill Layer** and selecting either Solid Color, Gradient, or Pattern, you may create a new fill layer.

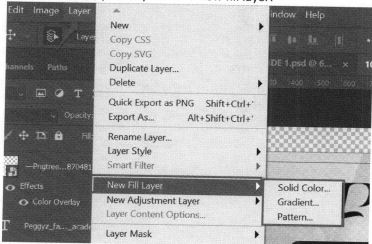

o **Shape layer**: Shapes created using the Shape Tools are stored in Shape Layers. Select the layer and Shape Tool to get editing options for a shape layer.

✦ **Empty Layers**: these are layers that have no elements in them. They are considered empty.

81

✦ **Adjustment Layers**: These layers allow you to apply adjustments to the layers beneath them, such as brightness or saturation, to the layers. Adjustment layers are a kind of non-destructive editing because they don't alter the source image.

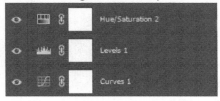

Layer Basics

The Layers panel lets you view, make, and modify layers. Although you can always go to **Window** > **Layers** to check it's on, this is typically located in the lower-right area of the screen.

By default, the Layer Panel is available in the main workspace. You may, however, reactivate it by hitting the f7 key on your keyboard if you misplace it. The layers panel will be used to control and alter the layers.

The image below displays the layers panels.

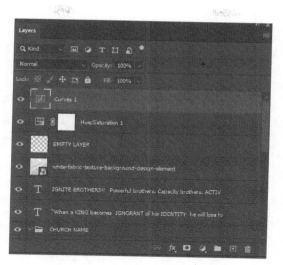

There are multiple components to the Photoshop Layers function. Let's look at each component and the different kinds of layers:

✦ **Thumbnail**: A thumbnail is a small image that contains the layer's content. It is visible on the layer.

✦ **Visibility Toggle**: In the layer panel, you can see each layer has an eye symbol. You can enable or disable the layer by clicking on the eye icon.

✦ **Layer Name**: This shows the name of the layer. By default, the name will be determined by the type of layer.
You can rename a layer by double-clicking its name, typing a new name, and then hitting the ENTER key.

✦ **Opacity and Fill**: The commands Opacity and Fill can be used to change a layer's opacity (or transparency). With one exception, both instructions work in the same way. Everything in the chosen layer will have its transparency altered by opacity.

Fill will alter the transparency of whatever is filling the layer, but it will disregard any applied effects.

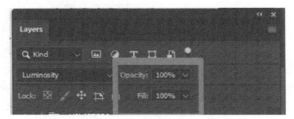

❖ **Blending Modes**: Blend modes affect how layers appear and are displayed. Each of the five groups of blending modes has a distinct effect on the layer. Combining blending modes and experimenting with different combinations is the simplest way to use them.

✦ **Locking Layers**: The option to lock layers in Photoshop can be helpful. There are multiple techniques to lock the layer or its contents. Each layer can be locked by selecting the layer and then the lock type. These are the many types of locks.

✦ **Layer Buttons:** For convenience and ease of use, several of these buttons perform tasks that are also accessible in other areas of the application but in the Layers Palette. A list of these buttons is shown below.

✦ **Link Layers**: Layers can be linked together by selecting two or more layers and clicking this button. They will all move together if they link.

✦ **Add a new layer style**: You can add a new layer style using this button without first going to Layer and choosing Layer Style from the menu.

✦ **Add Layer Mask**: The selected layer will receive a new layer mask when you click Add layer mask.

✦ **Create a new fill or adjustment layer**: By pressing this button, you can add a new layer style without using the Adjustments Palette.

✦ **Create a new group**: Creating a new group is as simple as clicking this (aka folder). To arrange the layers, drag them into this group.

✦ **Create a new layer**: A new, empty layer will be created when you click this.

✦ **Delete layer**: Select one or more layers and click on this button to delete.

Use the merge and flatten commands if you ever need to combine several layers or flatten the entire image.

Merge Layers
Merge Visible
Flatten Image

Follow the instructions below.

- After choosing the layers, right-click your mouse and select **Merge Selected** from the drop-down menu. All of the selected layers will be blended into one

- Combine or merge only visible layers () by selecting "**Merge Visible**" from the context menu.

- Right-click any layer's layer name, then choose "**Flatten Image**" to flatten the entire image.

Working with layers

As you are aware, the sequence in which layers are layered affects how your image looks. In order to change the layers' arrangement as needed, you must know how to shift them.

86

A layer's layer mask is a necessary component for non-destructive editing. The components of the image are shown and revealed by painting on the mask. Applying masks to a layer is a reversible way to hide a section of it. This method gives you more editing flexibility than deleting a layer entirely or just a section of it. To apply a layer mask to a layer, follow these steps:

- Select the layer you desire to mask
- Click on the layer mask icon (⬛) at the bottom of the layer panel.

Any area of a layer can be concealed by using a brush to paint black on the layer mask, and any previously hidden portion can be revealed by painting white on the layer mask. Black, white, and grey are the three colors that can be used to paint layer masks, and each has a distinct function.

- BLACK to conceal: When black is added to a layer mask, the contents of the layer beneath it are revealed while the layer containing the mask becomes invisible.
- WHITE to show: Adding white to a layer mask just makes the layer with the mask visible.
- To show the level of opacity, use GREY: The opacity of the layer with the mask changes when different shades of grey are added.

Photoshop is an advanced photo editor; usually, a new layer is created when we choose a new tool and start drawing on it. For example, if you use the text tool to add text to an image, a new layer will be created.

To manually add a new layer, press the **Ctrl + Shift + N keys** or click the new layer icon(⬛) located at the bottom of the layer panel. It will ask for a new layer, which you should name and then click **OK** to create. We can specify this layer's opacity, color, and color modes.

The method of deleting a layer is as simple as creating a new layer. Do the following to delete a layer.

- Right-click the layer in the **Layers Panel**.

⬧ Choose **Delete** from the drop-down menu or click on the **Delete icon** located at the bottom of the Layers panel().

In Photoshop, you must have at least one layer selected to carry out the majority of operations. Do the following to select the layer(s).

⬧ To choose a layer, just click on it in the Layers Panel. As seen on the right, a layer will turn blue when it is selected.

⬧ You can select multiple layers by holding down the CMD (Mac) or CTRL (Windows) key while clicking on each layer you wish to have selected.

⬧ To select multiple layers in sequence, choose the first layer, then hold down the SHIFT key and select the last layer.

You already know that the way your layers are arranged will affect the final appearance of your image. Layers must be able to be moved so that their arrangement can be altered as needed.

⬧ Choose the layer or layers you want to move.

✦ Click and hold down the mouse button to drag the layer to the desired spot. Between layers, a thick line will be displayed to show where the layer will be dropped. When the layer is where you want it to be, let go of the mouse button and it will go there.

A Photoshop project usually has several layers, which can quickly get complex and make it hard to find anything. Thankfully, there are several resources accessible to help identify different degrees.

✦ You can choose to search layers by **Kind, Name, Effect, Mode, Attribute**, or **Color** by clicking the Search Dropdown ().

✦ Use the options to the right of the **Search** Dropdown after choosing a search strategy to choose additional attributes to include in the search results.

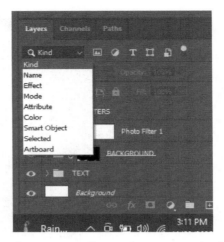

Another feature that can keep you and your layers organized is the option to create folders, sometimes known as groups. You are free to add layers to a group and organize them however you choose.

- By selecting the "**Create a new group**" button (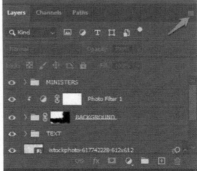) at the base of the layers palette, a new folder can be created.
- To include layers in the group, drag them onto the group folder layer.
- To rename the Group Name, double-click on it in the Layers Palette.

Right-click the layer group and choose **Ungroup Layers** to remove all of the layers from it. All of the layers will be ungrouped from the group, and the group will be deleted.

Do the following to change the size of your layers` thumbnails.

- Choose the Panel option (rectangular lines in the top-right corner) from the layer panel.

- then select the thumbnail size to modify the layer's thumbnail size.

90

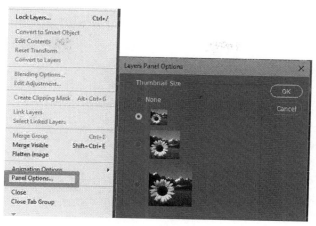

To change the contents of thumbnails, do the following.

✦ To change the thumbnail content, select the **Panel Options** from the Layers panel and select the entire document.

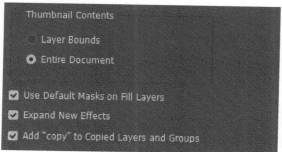

✦ Now, select the layer bounds to specify the thumbnail content on the layer.

To make several tweaks without impacting the original layer, we can duplicate a layer by following any one of these options.

✦ Right-click the layer and choose **"Duplicate Layer"** to make a copy of it.

◆ Select the layer you desire to duplicate, drag it, or use the arrow key as you hold the **Alt key (Window)/ Option key (macOS)**

◆ Select and drag the layer you desire to duplicate to the **create new layer icon (**  **)**

◆ Select the layer you want to copy and then use Ctrl J(Windows)/ Cmd J(macOS)

◆ Select your layer and use the copy-and-paste shortcut. Ctrl C to copy and Ctrl V to paste on Windows, Cmd C to copy, and Cmd V to paste on macOS.

It is possible to link two or more levels or groups. Until we unlink them, the relationship that is formed when layers are joined together will remain intact. We can apply or transfer transformation to linked layers.

◆ Select the layers or groups you want to link, then click the link icon at the bottom of the layer panel.

◆ Select the layers or groups you want to unlink, then click the link button once again. It will remove the layer links.

92

✦ The connected layers can be temporarily disabled. Temporarily shift-click the link icon to unlink them, then repeat the process to relink them.

To hide/show a layer, do the following.

✦ Click the eye icon next to the selected layers to make a layer invisible. Click on this symbol once more to reveal the layer.

Working with Adjustments Layers

Photoshop offers two options for editing and adjusting images or layers: **destructive** and **non-destructive**. A destructive edit modifies the original image data by making irreversible modifications to the image. Except for using Ctrl+Z to undo your activities, you can reverse the changes. Only when a layer mask is present may non-destructive edits create alterations to a project that are modifiable.

What are Adjustments Layers?

Adjustment Layers are a set of Photoshop editing tools that allow you to experiment with an image's color and tone without making permanent changes. Adjustment layers can easily be edited out to recover the original image. As the name suggests, adjustment layers are a unique type of Photoshop layer that lets you make changes to an image on one layer while maintaining the original image without completely changing it. Compared to direct alterations, adjustment layers offer you more freedom and control over image edits.

93

By default, an adjustment layer affects all layers below it, although you can change this behavior by clicking on the clipping icon() below the properties panel. When you create an adjustment layer, the Layers panel displays a white box representing the adjustment for that layer.

To use the Adjustment layers, follow either of the following procedures:

From the Layers panel

✦ Move down to the **Layer Panel** and **select** a circular logo with its semi-area-shaded black

✦ Select the adjustment you want to use.

From the Menu Bar

✦ Select **Layers** from the **Menu Panel**

✦ From the **Layer`s** display, Click on **New Adjustment Layers**

94

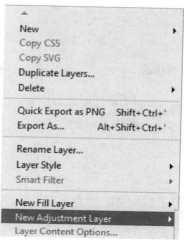

⇕ You can then choose the adjustment layer of your choice.

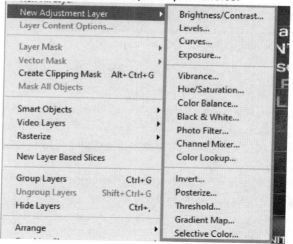

From the Adjustments Panel

⇕ Another way to access your Adjustment layers is to pick them from the **Adjustment Panel.** The Adjustment features in the **Adjustment Panel** are adjustment layers automatically.

Note that you can only access your Adjustment Panel if you have placed it in your workspace from the **Window** Option.

You may need to familiarize yourself with the terms below to know how some adjustment features operate.

- ✦ **Color grading**: Color grading in Photoshop is all about adjusting and making modifications to the colors and tones (levels of brightness) of an image.
- ✦ **Highlights:** consists of the brightest areas and it permits modifications to these areas
- ✦ **Shadow:** Unlike the Highlights, it consists of the darkest area of an image and allows changes to be made in these areas.
- ✦ **Mid-tones:** are areas that are between the darkest and the brightest areas, more like grey. Like the other features, Mid-tones also permit modifications to their areas.

Adjustment Presets
One of the most notable features added to Photoshop is Adjustment Presets. The same panels that contain the adjustment layers also contain them.

Adjustment Presets are already made effects created by Adobe to spice up user`s experience while working with Photoshop.

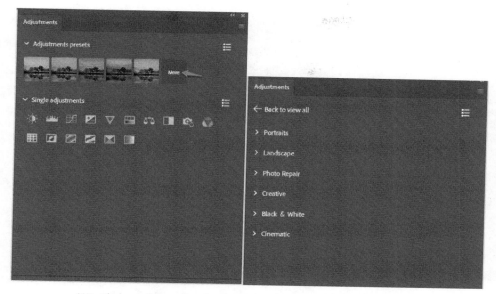

NB: Click on **"more"** to have access to all Adjustment Presets.

The Adjustment Presets in Photoshop are divided into **Portraits**, **Landscape**, **Photo Repair**, **Creative**, **Black and White**, and **Cinematic**.

Two or more adjustment layers comprise every adjustment preset. You can utilize adjustment presets more efficiently if you know how to use the adjustment layers. Come along with me as we explore further.

Adjustment Layers
Listed below are the adjustment layers available in Photoshop

Brightness/Contrast: This describes how light or dark an image is overall. A contrast is the variation in brightness between two items or places. This adjustment layer can be used to change an image's or photograph's brightness and contrast. To achieve it, adhere to the guidelines below.

- ⬍ Select **Brightness/Contrast** from the adjustment panel.

♦ Adjust the sliders to make edits to your desire.

Your image's highlights can be changed with the **brightness slider**, and the shadows may be changed with the **contrast slider**. Increasing the brightness makes every pixel lighter while increasing the contrast makes the dark sections darker and the dazzling parts lighter.

.

Levels: The levels tool can be used to adjust an image's colour balance and tone range. It does this by altering the brightness levels of the highlights, mid-tones, and shadows in your picture. Levels Presets are readily applied to additional photos after being saved. To utilise the Levels Adjustment, adhere to the guidelines provided below.

♦ Select "Levels" right from the adjustment panel,

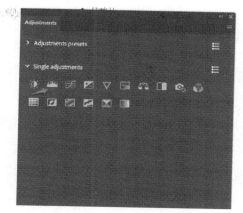

✦ You can make adjustments to your images in the levels panel by twerking the **eyedropper icons** and the **triangular icons** in the panel preview like it is in the image below.

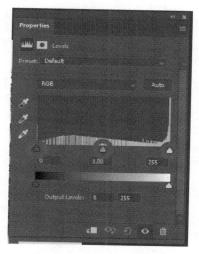

Curves: Although it is far more sophisticated and is used to alter a portion of an image rather than the entire image, this adjustment feature functions similarly to the levels. While the Levels adjustment enables you to proportionally alter all of the tones in your image, it lets you choose which area of the tonal scale you wish to alter. On the Levels graph, the shadows are displayed in the lower-left corner, while the highlights are displayed in the upper-right corner.

Use one of these adjustments (levels or curves) to change the tone of your image when the contrast is off (either too low or high).

The Levels Adjustment works well if you need to modify your tone generally. If you wish to make more targeted changes, you should use curves. This is relevant if you want to alter just the light or dark tones or a subset of the tonal range.

The steps listed below can be used to apply the curve correction,

- Select curve adjustment in the adjustment panel

- When you click the curves adjustment (see left), a graph with a diagonal line representing your image's tone range emerges. The image's initial values are shown on the x-axis, while the updated modified values are shown on the y-axis. A strip with a gradient from black to white that runs down each axis represents the image's tonal range.

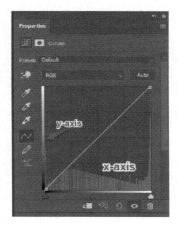

◆ To enhance the overall quality and contrast of your image, click to add points to the graph's line. Once a point has been added, you can move it up or down with your mouse. Pulling the point down will make your image darker, and pulling the point up will make it brighter.

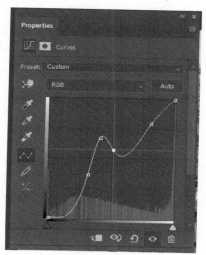

Exposure: This is the amount of light a photo is taken in. The exposure adjustment enables you to determine the amount of exposure in an image.

Select **Exposure** from the adjustment panel

You may adjust the exposure levels by using the Exposure, Offset, and Gamma sliders. Exposure will only change the image's highlights, the offset will only change the mid-tones, and gamma will only change the image's dark tones.

Vibrance: This is a brilliant feature that preserves the already intense colors while enhancing the intensity of the image's more muted tones. Furthermore, it prevents skin tones from being excessively saturated. Another aspect of the vibrance modification is the saturation control, which adjusts the intensity of every hue. **Saturation** can easily make colors and skin tones look odd. To adjust the image's saturation, it is recommended to utilize the **Hue/Saturation** adjustment instead of the Vibrance adjustment.

To use the Vibrance adjustment, follow the procedure below,

 ✦ Click on Vibrance in the adjustment panel

✦ This adjustment layer can be used to change an image's vibrance in two different ways. The **Saturation slider** evenly increases the saturation of each color in the picture. By focusing on the least saturated colors and avoiding oversaturating skin tones, the **Vibrance slider** subtly adjusts the saturation levels of every color.

Hue and Saturation: You may adjust your image's overall colour hue and saturation level with the aid of hue and saturation. It lets you alter a specific colour range or the full image's hue, saturation, and brightness.

Follow the procedures below, to use the Hue/Saturation adjustment.

✦ Select Hue/Saturation from the adjustment panel

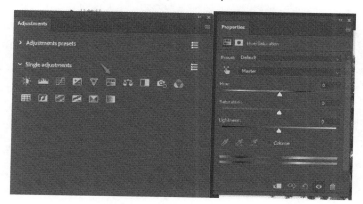

✦ You can change the hue (color) of the complete image by keeping "Master" in the dropdown menu (this is selected by default). Alternatively, you can name the particular color whose hue you wish to change. You can choose between reds, yellows, greens, cyan, blues, or magenta.

✦ You can deal with specific colors and modify the overall **lightness** of your image in addition to changing the image's obvious **hue** and color **saturation**. Remember that altering an image's overall saturation has an impact on your tonal range.

♦ The colorize feature in the hue/saturation adjustment allows you to change the colors in an image to a single color.

Color Balance: The Color Balance adjustment is used to provide general color correction. Finding a balance between two complementary colors is what is meant by using color balance. RGB colors, for example, go well with CMY colors. Cyan and red, magenta and green, and yellow and blue are examples of inversely complementary colors used in color balance. Therefore, if there is too much cyan in an image, the cyan value needs to be decreased, which will increase the red value. Avoid making too many changes to the color balance since you can unintentionally swap out one incorrect color for another.

Follow the procedure below, to use the color balance adjustment:

♦ Select Color Balance from the adjustment panel

✦ To determine the tonal range you want to modify, first choose either Shadows, Midtones, or Highlights.

✦ To maintain your luminosity values, select the Preserve Luminosity checkbox.

✦ You should move the slider towards the color you like to make brighter and away from the color you wish to make softer. Maintain the tonal balance even as your image's color changes.

Black and White: As the name implies, this adjustment layer allows it easy to add a color tint or convert your photographs to greyscale.

There are numerous methods for processing black-and-white photos. The black-and-white Photoshop Adjustment Layer is among the best. You can lighten or darken specific color ranges to enhance your black-and-white conversion. Toggle that slider, for example, to make the greens in your color image stand out more in the black-and-white version. You can change the contrast by making some colors lighter or darker.

- Select the black and white adjustment from the adjustment panel

- To improve your black-and-white conversion, you can make specific color ranges lighter or darker. For instance, if you want the blues in your color image to be more prominent in the black-and-white version, you can adjust that slider. By making some colors lighter or darker, you may change the contrast.

Photo Filter: Photo Filter adds many colour filters to your image. One quick and easy way to change a picture's mood or correct a colocolorur cast is to use Photoshop's Photo Filter Adjustment Layers. Although Photoshop offers you access to a far greater range of filter types, they are based on traditional filters from the days of film photography.

You can choose to use some of the popular filters at the preset density or roll your own. This is an easy-to-use tool, and I'll briefly go over the many options available to you so you may alter your photos and give some examples of how different settings could produce different effects.

To use the Photo Filter adjustment, follow the procedure below;

✦ Select Photo Filter from the adjustment panel

✦ It is simple to switch the filter by picking it from the list by clicking the drop-down menu adjacent to the **Filter button**. Simply select the **Filter button** if the drop-down is inactive and grayed out.

◆ You can choose the color of the filter if you want to get creative. This can be done by simply selecting the color box beneath the drop-down menu, which will bring up a new dialogue box called "Color Picker (Photo Filter Color)". This brings up the familiar Photoshop color picker, and when you select a new color, the drop-down menu turns grey and the Color button becomes active. You can see how your selected color affects your image in real-time.

✦ The Density slider makes it simple to adjust the filter strength. 25% is the default setting for this. Increase the amount of the new color added to the image by dragging this slider to the right. Decrease the effect by dragging it to the left for softer results.

✦ The Preserve Luminosity check box, the last parameter, maintains the overall brightness of your shot when selected.

Chanel Mixer: Any element in your image can be changed to any other colour in the rainbow with ease using the Channel Mixer adjustment layer, which is commonly used to produce high-quality conversions from colour to black and white, correct colour casts, and accentuate the colour. The adjustment layer allows you to easily mix the Red, Green, and Blue channels to change the colours of an image and also includes a monochrome mode to create black-and-white images.

Follow the procedure below, to use the Channel Mixer adjustment;

✦ Select the Channel Mixer in the adjustment panel

✦ Click on the drop-down menu adjacent to the **output channel** to select the channel you desire to modify.

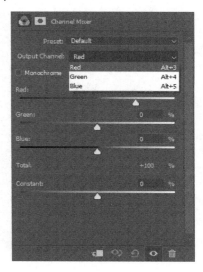

- Toggle the color sliders until you get your desired color or input a value in the rectangular box at the upper right of each slider to get the desired colors.

- It is necessary to keep an eye on each channel's overall value and aim to maintain it within 100%. Since exceeding 100% means that the color output is overly bright or dark and that you are losing data in the darkest or highlights, a warning is displayed. You are adding more color to the channel if the value is negative, and you are removing color if the value is positive.

Color Lookup: The color look-up adjustment layer unlocks the potential of look-up tables or LUTS. This powerful function enables you to move color information across programs and assign preset recipes to mimic various film stocks or produce complex color effects.

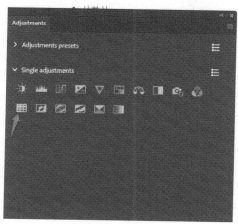

You can apply a variety of pre-packaged "looks" from this adjustment to your image. These many looks are loaded using three options: **3DLUT File, Abstract**, and **Device Link**.

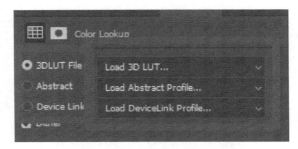

Every "look" remaps the colors in your image (LUT) using a lookup table. To style your photos, you may even create your LUTs in Adobe Speedgrade and then import them into Photoshop. These effects are intriguing.

Follow the instructions below to use the color lookup adjustment:

✦ Select the color lookup adjustment from the adjustment panel

✦ Pick a Color Lookup table from the list in the **Properties panel**. Pick a Color Lookup table from the list in the Properties panel.

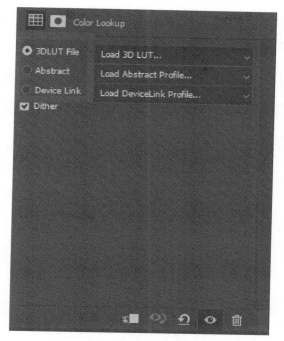

♦ From the Color Lookup table you selected, pick a preset and try out many presets to determine which one best suits your image.

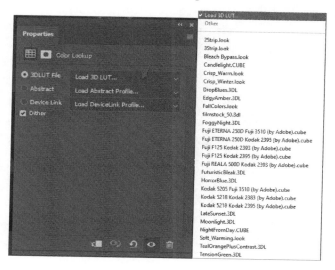

✦ To fine-tune the adjustment, use the Layers panel's Layer **Blend Mode** and **Opacity options.**

Invert: This adjustment layer flips the colors in your image to create a photo-negative appearance.

To use the invert adjustment layer, follow either of the instructions below

✦ Select the invert adjustment layer in the adjustment panel.

✦ Another way to use the invert adjustment is to add a layer mask to your image.

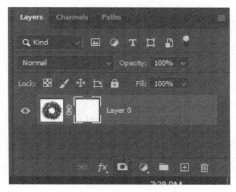

✦ Click on your layer mask.

✦ Then use the keyboard shortcut **Command + I (Mac)** or **Control + I (Windows)**

Posterize: With the help of this feature, you may assess the colour of the pixels in a particular region of an image and reduce the colour count without affecting the appearance of the original. This alteration gives pictures a painted-wood block-color look. The **Posterise Adjustment** Layer gives you a flat, poster-like look by restricting the brightness settings in your image.

.

You can adjust the amount of detail in an image by selecting the appropriate number on the levels slider. The higher the number, the more detail in your photograph. The lower the number, the less detail your image has.

This can be helpful if you want to screenprint your artwork. There are limitations to black and white tones.

Follow the instructions below to use the posterize adjustment.

✦ Select the posterize adjustment from the adjustment panel

117

♦ In the properties panel you will notice that the level slider is drastically reduced, toggle the slider or input the desired value till you are satisfied with the effect.

Threshold: Your photo is transformed into a monochrome (black-and-white) image with this tool. When you select Threshold from the list of Photoshop Adjustment Layers, your image becomes black and white. You can change the Threshold Level value to determine how many pixels are white or black.

To use the threshold adjustment, follow the procedure below;

♦ Select the threshold adjustment from the adjustment panel

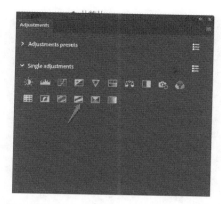

+ By toggling the Threshold Level value, you can select the number of pixels that are black or white till your desired result is obtained.

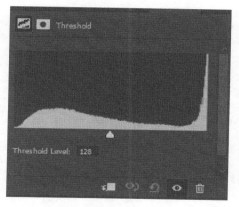

Selective Color: The strength of one primary colour in your image is changed by this adjustment layer, but the other primary colours remain unaltered. With this adjustment option, you may selectively alter the amount of process colour in each of an image's primary colour components. For example, you can change the Red color's CMYK value independently of the other colours in a picture. You can also eliminate colour in particular regions of your image by using selective color.

To use the selective color adjustment, follow the instructions below:

+ Select the selective color adjustment from the adjustment panel

✦ Click on the box adjacent to the color button to choose the primary color you want to modify.

✦ Toggle the color sliders to make adjustments to our image till you get your desired result.

Gradient Map: Unlike a gradient fill, which fills an area with a linear or radiant blend of colors, a gradient map applies the gradient by using the brightness and darkness values in the image as a map for how the gradient colors are applied. Adobe Photoshop's duotone effect is made possible by the effects. Images can be color-graded as overlays and color-replaced with several tones, typically two. Although black and white photographs are included in color replacement, this tool lets you select any two colors instead of the default two tones. To get the most out of this feature's duotone effect, you need first desaturate your image, depending on the type of outcome you want

To use the gradient map adjustment, follow the instructions below:

- Select the gradient map adjustment from the adjustment panel

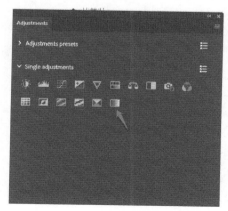

✦ There are several distinct gradients included with the Gradient Map tool, all of which may be customized in the gradient editor box. Click on the gradient fill, to pick the colors you want for it.

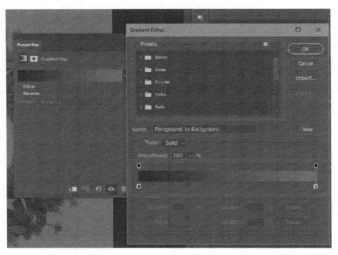

✦ If you desire to invert the colors of your gradient, check the **Reverse box** in the **gradient editor box**.

✦ Then click **OK** after you are satisfied with your result

The Three Auto-Commands

You may fix color, tone, and contrast imbalances in your photos with the use of the auto adjustment commands, which are one-tap instructions:

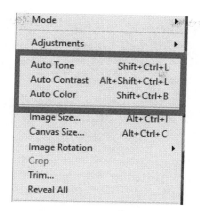

Photoshop has three built-in image adjustments: **Auto Tone**, **Auto Contrast**, and **Auto Color**. Each of these three Auto commands manipulates the color channels (these greyscale images) differently, producing different results. Because auto-image adjustments are completely automatic and execute their full functions as soon as they are selected, they are also referred to as auto-commands. Let's examine each auto command in brief.

Understanding How the Auto Contrast, Auto Tone, And Auto Color Operate
It can be useful to know why one of the three Auto commands performed better than the others, even though using them doesn't technically need a comprehension of their mechanics. To really understand how the Auto commands work, we need to have a fundamental understanding of Photoshop's color channels.

The basic colors of light are these three primary hues, from which all other colors are derived in some way. White is created by combining red, green, and blue in equal amounts and at their highest intensities. Red, green, and blue are used in some combination to create every shade and color between black and white. All three of the primary colors are completely absent in black. For example, yellow can be made by combining red and green. Combining red and blue results in magenta, whereas combining green and blue results in cyan. When all of the red, green, and blue hues are combined, there are millions, if not billions, of colors.

Photoshop blends the three primary colors using color channels. Red, green, and blue are the three channels that are available. The Channels panel, which by default is adjacent to the Layers panel, contains these color channels. Open the tab at the top of the panel group to gain access to it:

123

The Red, Green, and Blue channels are visible in this image, coupled with what appears to be a fourth channel, RGB at the top, But don't be misled by the RGB channel. It hardly even qualifies as a channel. Red, Green, and Blue, or RGB, is the simple composite of the Red, Green, and Blue channels, which together provide our full-color image:

You might be surprised to learn that the preview thumbnails for the Red, Green, and Blue channels don't display any color at all! Instead, each one is a greyscale image. In fact, if we look at them more attentively, we can see that each channel has a different greyscale image. To view a preview of each channel as it will look in your document, just click on it.

Photoshop determines how many colors to add to each region based on the greyscale image's brightness values. Because it illustrates how the color in each channel is blended with it, the greyscale in each color channel differs somewhat from the others. For example, in the Red Channel, the full-color version has more red added to the brighter sections and less red mixed into the darker areas. Black portions in the greyscale image have no Red at all, whereas pure white areas have pure Red added to them.

Green is subtracted from areas of greater darkness and added to areas of greater brightness in the Green Channel. parts that are completely black have no green at all, while any parts that are white get intense green injections.

124

In the full-color version of the Blue Channel, lighter areas display locations where more blue is mixed in, while darker areas receive less blue. Full-intensity blue is applied to areas of pure white. There is absolutely no blue in pure black places. Generally speaking, the channel with the darkest patches is the Blue Channel.

Auto Contrast.

Auto Contrast is the most basic and straightforward of the three. When we select Auto Contrast, Photoshop simply turns the darkest pixels into pure black and the lightest into pure white, redistributing all intermediate tonal values in between. This is because Photoshop treats all three color channels as though they were a single greyscale image. The result of this procedure is an image with improved overall contrast. Because Auto Contrast sees all three color channels as a single composite image, it is important to keep in mind that it does not change the image's colors. It only adds contrast overall, so it's a good choice for photos that don't have any color problems but just need a little more "pop."

To use the Auto Contrast adjustment, follow the procedure below:

- Open the **Image Menu** from the **Menu Bar** and select **Auto contrast.** The command carries out the operation immediately.

125

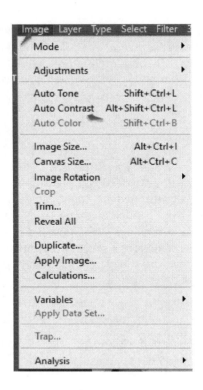

Auto Tone

The only notable distinction between Auto Contrast and Auto Tone is that Auto Tone also redistributes all other tonal values in between, turning the lightest pixels into pure white and the darkest into pure black. Because it performs this channel-by-channel, the Red, Green, and Blue channels each receive a distinct spike in contrast. Since Photoshop uses the brightness values in each color channel to decide how much of each hue to mix into the whole color, we can effectively change how the colors are blended by adjusting the color channels independently of one another. This indicates that Auto Tone alters the image's color as opposed to Auto Contrast, which just improves overall contrast. Auto Tone might be able to remove any unwanted color cast from your image. Unfortunately, Auto Tone might end up adding a color cast to an image that didn't have one at first.

- Open the Image Menu from the Menu Bar and select Auto Tone

126

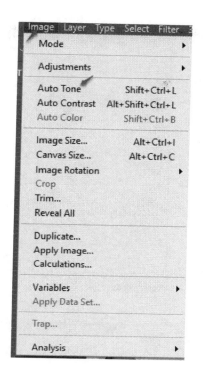

Auto Color

Auto Tone and Auto Color are connected. Since it also alters the darkest and lightest pixels in each channel individually from white to black and from black to darkest to lightest, the Red, Green, and Blue channels are once more impacted independently and separately from one another. But Auto Color takes it a step further. Instead of just redistributing all the other tonal values in between, it tries to correct any unwanted color cast by neutralizing the image's mid-tones. Because of this, Auto Color is usually (though not always) the best choice for enhancing contrast and resolving color problems at the same time.

To use the Auto Color adjustment on your work, Open the **Image Menu** from the **Menu Bar** and select **Auto Color**.

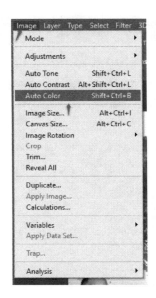

Blending Modes in Photoshop

Blending modes are mathematical formulas that mix layers by considering color, saturation, brightness, or a combination of these.

Blending modes allow you to apply textures, overlays, or target alterations to certain areas of your image without the need for layer masks. It is strongly advised to employ Blending Modes to create nondestructive effects. The blend you apply only changes the visual result. The Blending Mode can be reversed or changed at any time. The blending mode may be found next to the opacity slider in the upper-left corner of the layer panel.

Blend Modes require a minimum of two layers to work. The layer above is called Blend, and the layer below is called Base. The Blending Mode determines the mix operation applied to the mix layer.

By default, all layers are set to Normal, and groups are set to Pass Through.

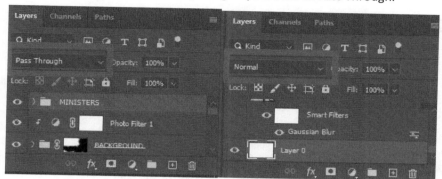

There are 27 blend modes in Photoshop and they are grouped into six categories. Each group of blending modes is categorized based on similar operations that they perform and they are; **Normal Modes**, **Darken Modes**, **Lighten Modes**, **Contrast Modes**, **Comparative Modes**, and **Composite Modes**.

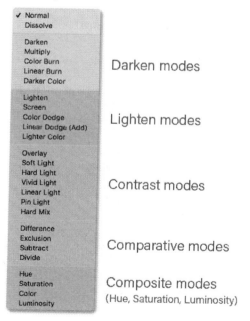

(Image source from https://www.photoshopessentials.com/photo-editing/layer-blend-modes/intro/)

Understanding Each Blending Mode for their uniqueness

Before we move into each blending mode, let`s quickly discuss an important aspect of blending modes; **Neural Colors**.

- **Neural Colors**: Neutral Colors are colors that blend without making any difference, and are offered by some blending modes. Shades of grey are another name for neural colors.

  For example, White is the Neutral Color for the Multiply Blending Mode. Any white pixels on a layer will become translucent when using Multiply. The neutral color for the Screen Blending Mode is black. Any black pixels on a layer will become translucent when using the Screen.

Normal Blending Modes

The blending methods used by the blending modes in this category do not combine pixels. Instead, the mix between layers is controlled by the Opacity slider.

- **Normal:** When it comes to Photoshop layers, the default Blending Mode is "Normal." In the absence of any algorithms or arithmetic, opaque pixels will mask the pixels beneath them. You must reduce the Opacity in order to expose or "blend" the pixels with the layer underneath.

  Shortcut on the keyboard: Alt Shift N (Windows) or Option Shift N (Mac) (macOS).

  Neutral Colors: None
- **Dissolve**: Furthermore, the dissolve blending option does not blend pixels. Dissolve simply makes the pixels underneath visible when the layer's Opacity or Fill is reduced. Dissolve always shows the base color and never a combination of two colors. If anti-aliasing is not used, the effect will look grainy and harsh. The pixels underneath are shown by a pseudo-random noise dither pattern whose intensity varies with opacity.

  Keyboard shortcuts: Alt Shift I (Windows) or Option Shift I (macOS)

  Neutral Colors: none

Darken Blending Modes

As the name implies, the Blending Modes under the Darken category will make the final product's colors darker.

White is a neutral color for every Blend Mode in this category. White pixels will become translucent when anything darker than white is present, and the pixels beneath it will become darker when anything lighter than white is present.

- **Darken**: The Darken Blending Mode selects the base color or blend color based on which RGB channel has the darker brightness values. In this mixing option, the darkest of the two colors is retained after comparing the base and blend colors. Pixels are not merged. If the colors of the base layer and the blend layer are the same, nothing changes.
  Keyboard Shortcut: Alt Shift K (Windows) or Option Shift K (macOS)
  Neutral Colors: White
  * Not available in the Lab Color Space.
- **Multiply**: One of the most used Blending Modes in Photoshop is multiply. You have probably used it a lot already. With this Blending Mode, the blend color increases the luminosity of the base color. There is always a darker color as a result. Black pixels remain unchanged when white is present.
  Depending on the blend layer's luminosity values, multiply can result in a wide range of darkening levels. A wonderful Blending Mode for shadows or dimming pictures is *Multiply*.
  Keyboard Shortcut: Alt Shift M (Windows) or Option Shift M (macOS)
  Neutral Colors: White
- **Color Burn**: By raising the contrast between the base and blend colors, the Color Burn Blending Mode produces a darker image than Multiply, with more intensely saturated mid-tones and fewer highlights.
  Keyboard Shortcut: Alt Shift B (Windows) or Option Shift B (macOS)
  Neutral Colors: White
  * Not available in the Lab Color Space or 32-Bi32-bit.
- **Linear Burn**: Based on the value of the blend color, Linear Burn reduces the brightness of the base color. The outcome is less saturated than Color Burn but darker than Multiply. Compared to the other Blending Modes in the Darken category, Linear Burn also produces the most contrast in darker colors.
  Keyboard Shortcut: Alt Shift A (Windows) or Option Shift A (macOS)
  Neutral Colors: White
  * Not available in 32-Bi32-bit.
- **Darker Color**: Darker Color Blending Mode and Darken are extremely similar. Pixels are not blended in this blending mode. The darkest of the two is kept and just the base and blend colors are compared.
  Darker Color examines the sum of all the RGB channels, whereas **Darken** examines each RGB channel separately before blending them.
  Keyboard Shortcut: None
  Neutral Colors: White
  * Not available in the Grayscale Mode.

131

Lighten Blending Modes

The Blending Modes in this area are either the opposite of or complementary to those in the Darken category. Using the Lighten Blending Modes will produce brighter colors. Black is a neutral color for every Blend Mode in this category. Anything darker than black will make the pixels beneath it brighter, whereas any color lighter than black will make the black pixels transparent.

- **Lighten**: The lightest of the two bases and blend colors are retained when using the Lighten Blending Mode. If the two colors match, then nothing changes. Lighten blends the pixels by taking into account each of the three RGB channels separately, similar to the Darken blend mode.
  Keyboard Shortcut: Alt Shift G (Windows) or Option Shift G (macOS)
  Neutral Colors: None
  * Not available in the Lab Color Space.
- **Screen**: Another of Photoshop's most used Blending Modes is Screen. Always a brighter hue is the end outcome. While the brighter pixels remain the same, black becomes transparent.
  The screen is an excellent Blending Mode for brightening photos or adding highlights because it may provide a wide range of brightness levels depending on the luminosity values of the blend layer.
  Keyboard Shortcut: Alt Shift S (Windows) or Option Shift S (macOS)
  Neutral Colors: Black
  * Not available in 32-Bi32-bit.
- **Color Dodge**: By reducing the contrast between the base and blend colors, the Color Dodge Blending Mode produces a brighter appearance than Screen, producing saturated mid-tones and blown-out highlights.
  Keyboard Shortcut: Alt Shift D (Windows) or Option Shift D (macOS)
  Neutral Colors: Black
  * Not available in the Lab Color Space or 32-Bi32-bit.
- **Linear Dodge (Add)**: Compared to Screen or Color Dodge, Linear Dodge (Add) yields effects that are comparable but stronger. This blending mode examines the color data in each channel and boosts the brightness of the base color to reflect the blend color. Nothing changes when black is blended in.
  Keyboard Shortcut: Alt Shift W (Windows) or Option Shift W (macOS)
  Neutral Colors: Black
- **Lighter Color**: Lighter Color and Lighten are pretty similar. Pixels are not blended in this blending mode. Only the base and blend colors are compared, and only the brighter of the two is kept.

To create a final blend, Lighten looks at each RGB channel, whereas Lighter Color examines the composite of all the RGB channels.
Keyboard Shortcut: Alt Shift (Windows) or Option Shift (macOS)
Neutral Colors: Black
* Not available in the Grayscale Mode.

Contrast Blending Modes
The Blending Modes in this category are a cross between the Lighten and Darken categories.
Whether the colors are darker or lighter than 50% grey is decided by Photoshop. When the color is more than 50% grey, Photoshop employs the Darkening Blending Mode. When the color is more vibrant than 50% grey, Photoshop employs the Brightening Blending Mode.

50% gray is a Neural Color for all Blend Modes in this category, except Hard Mix.

- **Overlay**: Another of the most widely used Blending Modes in Photoshop is Overlay. On colors that are brighter than 50% gray, Screen is used at half power. Additionally, on colors that are darker than 50% gray, multiply at half strength. 50% gray turns translucent in and of itself. You should be aware that "half-strength" does not refer to opacity at 50%. Consider altering mid-tones as another way to think about overlay. Light tones shift the mid-tones to brighter colors, while dark tones shift them to darker colors

  Overlay and the other Contrast Blending Modes differ from one another in that it base their calculations on the brightness of the colors in the base layer. The brightness of the blend layer serves as the foundation for all other contrast blending modes' calculations.
  Keyboard Shortcut: Alt Shift O (Windows) or Option Shift O (macOS)
  Neutral Colors: 50% Gray
  * Not available in 32-bit Mode.
- **Soft Light**: Overlay and Soft Light are extremely similar. Depending on the luminance levels, it either applies a darkening or a brightening effect, albeit much more subtly.

  Consider Soft Light to be a gentler variation of Overlay without the jarring contrast.
  Keyboard Shortcut: Alt Shift F (Windows) or Option Shift F (macOS)
  Neutral Colors: 50% Gray
  * Not available in 32-bit Mode.
- **Hard Light**: Making its computations, Hard Light mixes the Multiply and Screen utilizing the brightness values of the Blend layer. The base layer is used in the overlay. Hard Light typically produces powerful results, and you'll frequently need to lower the Opacity to achieve better ones.

133

Although Hard Light could seem to share certain similarities with Soft Light, this is untrue. They are a component of the first group of computed blending modes and are considerably more closely related to overlay.
Keyboard Shortcut: Alt Shift H (Windows) or Option Shift H (macOS)
Neutral Colors: 50% Gray
* Not available in 32-bit Mode.

✥ **Vivid Light**: Vivid Light can be compared to an extreme form of Overlay and Soft Light. Anything that is 50% gray or lighter is brightened, while anything that is 50% gray or darker is darkened. Vivid Light produces a strong result, therefore you'll probably need to lower Fill or Opacity.
The fifth of the eight special blending modes, called Vivid Light, blends differently depending on whether Fill or Opacity is changed.
Keyboard Shortcut: Alt Shift V (Windows) or Option Shift V (macOS)
Neutral Colors: 50% Gray

✥ **Linear Light**: Linear Light employs a combination of Linear Dodge (Add) and Linear Burn on lighter and darker pixels, respectively. Since Linear Light produces a powerful result, you will probably need to lower Fill or Opacity. Linear Light employs a combination of Linear Dodge (Add) and Linear Burn on lighter and darker pixels, respectively. Since Linear Light produces a powerful result, you will probably need to lower Fill or Opacity.
Keyboard Shortcut: Alt Shift J (Windows) or Option Shift J (macOS)
Neutral Colors: 50% Gray
* Not available in the Lab Color Space or 32-bit Mode.

✥ **Pin Light**: Pin Light is an aggressive Blending Mode that simultaneously blends Darken and Lightens. It eliminates any mid-tones
Keyboard Shortcut: Alt Shift Z (Windows) or Option Shift Z (macOS)
Neutral Colors: 50% Gray
* Not available in 32-bit Mode. mid-tones and can produce patches or blotches.

✥ **Hard Mix**: Hard Mix applies the blend by adding the value of each RGB channel of the blend layer to the corresponding RGB channels in the base layer. The resulting image loses a lot of detail, and the color choices are limited to black, white, or one of the six primary colors (yellow, cyan, magenta, or cyan).
Keyboard Shortcut: Alt Shift L (Windows) or Option Shift L (macOS)
Neutral Colors: None
* Not available in 32-bit Mode.

Inversion Blending Modes
The inversion blending modes look for variations between the base and blend layers to create the blend.

❖ **Difference**: The difference between the base and blend pixels is used as the blend in the Difference Blending Modes. The colors of the base layer are reversed by white. It produces the same outcome as pressing Ctrl I (Windows) or Command I to invert the colors of the base layer (macOS).

Dark grays slightly darken the image whereas black produces no change. For aligning layers with related information, this blending mode might be of great assistance. The outcome will become dark if two pixels are identical.

Keyboard Shortcut: Alt Shift E (Windows) or Option Shift E (macOS)

Neutral Colors: Black

* Not available in the Lab Color Space.

❖ **Exclusion**: Exclusion and Difference are extremely similar. While blending with black results in no change, blending with white flips the values of the base colors. On the other hand, blending with 50% gray results in 50% gray.

Keyboard Shortcut: Alt Shift X (Windows) or Option Shift X (macOS)

Neutral Colors: Black

* Not available in the Lab Color Space or 32-bit Mode.

❖ **Subtract**: The base layer's pixel values are subtracted when using the Subtract Blending Mode. By reducing brightness, this Blending Mode severely darkens pixels.

White has no impact. The outcome only becomes darker as the blend values increase brighter. Observe how the gradient's light portions are nearly pure black, whereas its dark areas just slightly changed. The results of Subtract and Divide are the exact opposite.

Keyboard Shortcut: None

Neutral Colors: Black

* Not available in the Lab Color Space.

❖ **Divide**: Divide converts each color into a percentage. White emerges from blending with the same color since any number divided by itself equals 1, or 100%. Due to the indefinite nature of diving by zero, black (0%) gives you black. Nothing changes. Divide has the exact opposite result as subtract.

White does nothing. The result only becomes brighter as the blend values go darker. While the light portions of the blend layer make a relatively tiny change, the dark areas of the blend layer produce brilliant hues. Divide produces the same outcome as flipping the Blend layer and selecting Color Dodge as the Blend Mode.

Keyboard Shortcut: None

Neutral Colors: White

* Not available in the Lab Color Space.

Component Blending Modes

The component blending modes combine the primary color components' hue, saturation, and brightness to create the mix.

The component group's Blend Modes are not available in the Grayscale Mode.

- ✦ **Hue**: The basic colors' brightness and saturation are preserved while the hue of the blend colors is kept.

  If the neutral gray base layer, the hue won't make a difference. With the Hue Blend Mode, a layer's colors could be altered while the original's tones and saturation were kept.

  Keyboard Shortcut: Alt Shift U (Windows) or Option Shift U (macOS)

  Neutral Colors: None

  * Not available in the Grayscale Mode.

- ✦ **Saturation**: The hue and luminosity of the base colors are affected by the saturation of the blend colors in the saturation blending mode (details). If the base layer is a neutral gray, saturation won't make a difference.

  Because none of the pixels contain saturation, a black-and-white blend layer will make the image black and white.

  Keyboard Shortcut: Alt Shift T (Windows) or Option Shift T (macOS)

  Neutral Colors: None

  * Not available in Grayscale Mode.

- ✦ **Color**: The base colors' brightness (details) are affected by the hue and saturation of the blend colors when using the Color Blending Mode.

  For coloring monochromatic photographs, the Color Blending Mode works well. The second set of computed blending modes is color and luminance. You will receive the same outcome if you apply the Luminosity Blending Mode on the base layer, then reverse the order of the layers, as you will if you apply the Color Blending Mode to the blend layer.

  Keyboard Shortcut: Alt Shift C (Windows) or Option Shift C (macOS)

  Neutral Colors: None

  * Not available in Grayscale Mode.

- ✦ **Luminosity**: The hue and saturation of the base color are altered by the brightness (detail) of the mixed colors.

  The second set of computed blending modes is luminance and color.

  Keyboard Shortcut: Alt Shift Y (Windows) or Option Shift Y (macOS)

  Neutral Colors: None

  * Not available in Grayscale Mode.

Improving your Designs with Layer Styles

Several layer effects combined to create a more complete look is called a **Layer Style**. Layer styles further comprise the blend mode, current Opacity and Fill Opacity settings and any Blending Options that have been applied to the layer. Drop Shadow, Stroke, Outer Glow, and other particular effects are called **Layer Effects**. It's common to use layer styles and layer effects interchangeably.

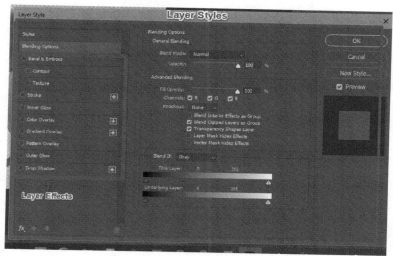

Use either of these methods to access the layer style`s window

❖ You may access the Layer Style dialog box by selecting **Blending Options** from the context menu when you right-click on your layer.

❖ You may access the Layer Style window by double-clicking on the thumbnail preview of your layer in the Layers Panel.

♦ From the **Menu Bar**, Select **Layer Style**.

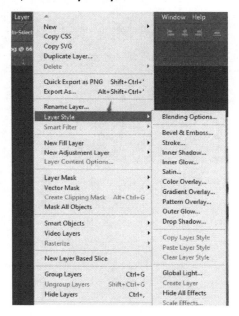

♦ Lastly, you may want to access your layer-style dialog window from your layer panel by clicking on the layer effects icon (*fx*)

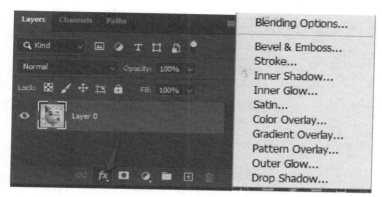

Preset Styles

Photoshop comes with pre-made layer styles that are known as preset styles. Just select a layer style by clicking on it, and the effect will be applied immediately to your layer.

To access the preset styles in Photoshop, follow either of these procedures.

✦ From the **Windows Menu** in the **Menu Bar**, Select **Styles**, and the style panel pops up afterward.

✦ You may also access them from the **layer styles dialog window**

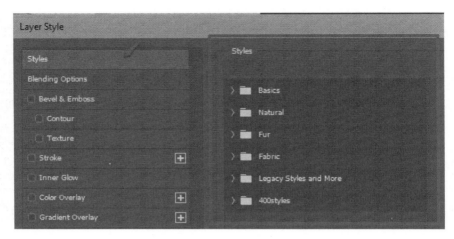

Layer Effects

Layer effects are a collection of editable, non-destructive effects in Photoshop that may be applied to almost any kind of layer. Although there are 10 different layer effects, they may be categorized into three main groups: **Strokes** & **Overlays**, and **Shadows** and **Glows**. Live effects that are directly connected to the layers they are applied to are called layer effects. As a result, if you modify the contents of a layer, any effects that have been applied to it will update instantly.

With text, graphics, and vector forms, layer effects can be applied to create realism or uniqueness in ways that would be difficult, if not impossible, without them.

You may apply many effects to a single layer, toggle them on and off, adjust their parameters, and remove layer effects without permanently changing your image. You may even add layer effects to a complete layer group to apply the same effects to multiple layers simultaneously. Additionally, you may combine type and layer effects to create amazing text effects while maintaining complete editability for your content.

Below are the layer effects in Photoshop

⬧ **Bevel & Emboss**: This layer effect makes your layer appear "popped out" or "pressed in" by applying both highlights and shadows.

⬧ **Stroke**: The Stroke effect will use your chosen color, pattern, or gradient to outline your whole layer.

* **Inner Shadow**: The Inner Shadow effect adds a shadow to your layer's inner edges, giving them a recessed appearance.

* **Inner Glow**: The inner boundaries of your layer will be illuminated with the Inner Glow effect.

* **Satin**: Utilizing internal shading, the satin effect gives your layer a glossy appearance. For generating effects like fabric and glass, use this effect.

* **Color Overlay**: Any color you choose will fill your layer when using the Color Overlay effect. Both subtle and drastic color changes can be achieved using this technique.

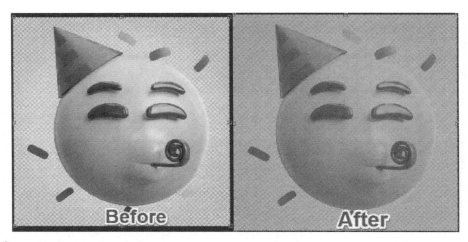

✦ **Gradient Overlay**: With the Gradient Overlay effect, at least two colors of your choice will be filled into your layer and seamlessly blended.

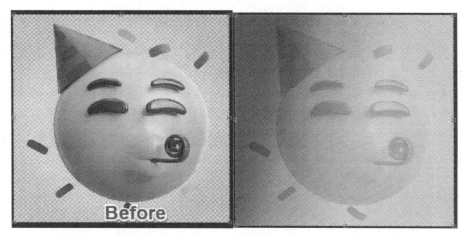

✦ **Pattern Overlay**: Your layer will be filled with the pattern of your choice if you use the Pattern Overlay effect.

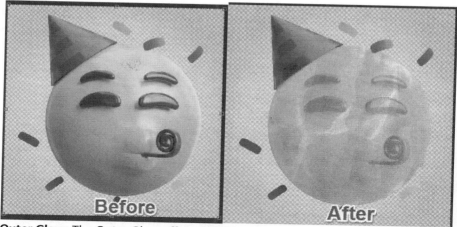

- **Outer Glow**: The Outer Glow effect will shine a light on your layer's outer edge.

- **Drop Shadow**: The shadow behind your layer will be added using the drop shadow effect.

CHAPTER SIX

SELECTING AND MASKING IN PHOTOSHOP

What you will learn in this chapter.

- **Photoshop selection techniques.**
- **How to use Photoshop Selection tools.**
- **How to mask a selection.**
- **How to refine a selected area.**

Starting with Selection and Selection Tools

A selection is an area you choose from an image. When you choose an area, you can change it (for instance, you can lighten one section of a picture without changing the others). One can use a **selection tool** or a **selection command** to produce a selection. A selection border surrounds the selection and can be hidden. You cannot work with any areas outside the selection border until the selection is deselected, but you can change, copy, or remove pixels inside the selection border.

Adobe Photoshop provides selection tools for several types of selections. The Magic Wand tool, for example, enables a one-click selection of an area with matching colors, while the Elliptical Marquee tool picks elliptical and circular areas. More complex selections can be made with one of the Lasso tools. The edges of a selection can even be softened with feathering and anti-aliasing. Every selection tool, with the exception of the marquee tools, functions well using the Color Algorithm. In this section, we will look at twelve of Photoshop's most important selection tools. We'll explain the features of each command and tool and provide tips on how to make the most of them.

On the toolbar, a lot of Photoshop's selection tools are nestled among related tools. The selection tools are located in the Tools panel, which is by default on the left side of your screen.

The three nests of selection tools present in the Tool Bar are **The Marquee Tools, The Lasso Tools,** and **The Object Selection Tools**.

The Marquee Tools

The Marquee Tools nest are **Rectangular Marquee Tool, Elliptical Marquee Tool, Single Row Marquee Tool,** and **Single Column Marquee Tool**.

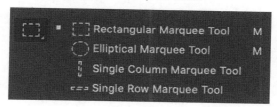

Using the Marquee tools, you can drag a shape over an area to select it. You can use a rectangle marquee tool, an elliptical marquee tool, or two single-line forms. Click and drag the shape to the desired size after selecting the marquee you want to use. The decision appears when you release it. Holding down the Shift key while dragging creates a square or circle by default, dragging from a corner. Holding down the **Alt key (Windows)** or Option key (macOS) will draw a shape that begins in the center.

In the **Options Bar**, you can change the style from Normal to Fixed Ratio. Consequently, a circle or square is created. Another option is to choose a fixed size, which is a choice of a predefined size.

When you choose a selection tool, more options appear in the **Options Bar**. These options include a set of icons that illustrate how various selections will work together.

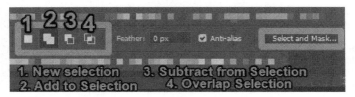

- A Square ⬛ (New Selection) allows you to draw a new selection
- The Overlapping Squares ⬛ (Add to Selection) allows you to add to previous selections
- A filled and an empty square ⬛ (Subtract from selection): allows you to remove the new selection from the previous one. Another way to use this feature is to hold the Alt Key (Windows) or Option Key (macOS) while making a new selection.
- The Second Overlapping Square (Overlap Selection): allows you to keep the area shared by the new and previous selections.

Other options in the Options Bar Include;

- **Feather**: This makes the selection and its surroundings blend seamlessly.
- **Select And Mask**: The Select and Mask button will create a masking layer based on your choices. Alt key + Ctrl R (Windows) and Option key + Cmd R (macOS) are shortcuts.

Note: that some of these features are available in all of the selection tools.

The Lasso Tools
The Lasso Tools nests three other selection tools and they are **Lasso Tool, Polygonal Lasso tool,** and **Magnetic Lasso Tool.**

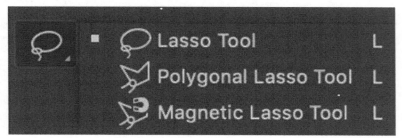

- **Lasso Tool**: This tool allows you to choose an object by drawing a free-form lasso around it. It is not a very accurate gadget. Use it when you want to make a broad decision.
- **Polygonal Lasso Tool**: The Polygonal Lasso selects only straight-lined geometric shapes. These could be more complex shapes than just squares or rectangles. Click and drag along the edge of a form to create a line. You can turn a corner with just one click. The tool lets you change the direction and stops the line there. Then, while holding down the Shift key, drag to draw a line, either vertically or horizontally. The chosen shape is complete when you double-click or return to the beginning.
- **Magnetic Lasso Tool**: The Lasso tool and the Magnetic Lasso tool work in a similar way. Drawing around an object is the first step in selecting it. The line is drawn to edges like a magnet to help you make a more accurate choice as you create. This tool works well for you when an object has multiple curves. There should be a clickable edge on the item you wish to choose. Next, drag the line around the shape. Pins begin to show up when a tool locks onto an edge. The selection shape is complete when you double-click or click where you initially clicked.

  The magnetic instrument has a round shape. You can see this more clearly if you turn on Caps Lock. Photoshop looks for a border inside the circle. The circle gets larger when the choices bar's width is increased. To aid the algorithm in finding an advantage, you can also alter the contrast. Frequency is the number of pins placed along the edge. You can change this to show more or fewer pins. However, you can click to add a pin at any time along the line.

Object Selection Tools

In this tool nest are **Object Selection, Quick Selection Tool,** and **Magic Wand Tool.**

- **Object Selection**: In 2019, Adobe included this in Photoshop. At first glance, it seems much like the Marquee tool. To choose an object, first draw a lasso or rectangle around it. After that, Photoshop looks through the shape's contents to find any objects. The subject-specific program then further refines the selection.

- **Quick Selection**: The Quick Selection tool is a fast way to select a well-defined object. Click inside an object to choose it. Before extending the selection to include similar pixels, Photoshop searches for borders and colors. To include another portion of the object in the selection, click on it. Alternatively, use the cursor to paint in the selection.

The Quick Selection tool functions similarly to a brush tool. You can change the brush stroke's size, angle, hardness, and spacing. Click the Plus icon to add to the selection. Holding down the chosen key or clicking the minus sign will erase a piece of the selection.

- **Magic Wand**: Color selection should be done using the Magic Wand tool. You can click on any color in your image to make all of its instances stand out. Tolerance in the Options bar modifies the level of accuracy in the color selection.

With low tolerance levels, the color selection is precise. When the tolerance is greater, the algorithm selects colors that are comparable to the one you selected. Click a second color to expand the selection. Holding down the option key while clicking a color will remove it from the choices.

If the Contiguous box is left unchecked, the colors are selected for the entire frame. Only colors that are similar to the selected color are available when the Contiguous checkbox is used. If the **Contiguous box** is left unchecked, the colors are selected for the entire frame. Only colors that are similar to the selected color are available when the Contiguous checkbox is used.

Not all the selection tools available in Photoshop are kept in the Tool Bar, Photoshop has a **Select Menu** in the **Menu Bar**. Selection tools are some of the options. Others modify the selection tools nested in the Tool Bar

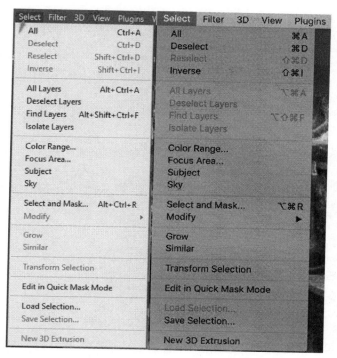

- **All**: this is a command that allows you to select all parts of a layer. Shortcut =Ctrl/Cmd + A
- **Deselect**: this is a command that permits you to deselect every selection in a layer. Shortcuts = Ctrl/Cmd D
- **Reselect: this** is a command that allows you to reselect previous selections. Shortcut = Shift+ Ctrl/Cmd + D
- **Inverse:** this command allows you to inverse your selection, that is, it deselects your original selection and selects the parts that are outside your selection. Shortcut = Shift + Ctrl/Cmd + I

Other Selection tools in the Select Menu are **Select Subject**, **Select Sky**, **Color Range**, **Focus Area**, and **Select and Mask**.

Select Object

The Select Subject tool is comparable to the Object Selection tool. But it's easier to use. Photoshop identifies possible subjects by analyzing your image. Although this selection tool isn't always perfect, you can use another tool, such as the lasso tool, to refine your pick if it's not perfect. To utilize the **Select Subject** function,

- Click on **Select** in the **Menu Bar**
- From the Select drop-down menu click on **Subject**

Another way to access the Select Subject feature is to access it from the **Object Selection Tools`** Options Bar.

Select Sky

The sky had to be manually masked before Adobe included a Sky Replacement feature in Photoshop. The task was made easier by this selection tool. Even in the presence of distractions, such as green trees, Photoshop can identify the sky.

To access this selection tool,

- Click on **Select** in the **Menu Bar**
- Select **Sky** in the **Select** drop-down menu.

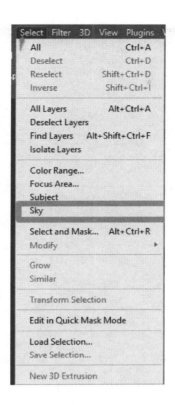

Color Range

The Magic Wand and Color Range tools can also be used similarly. The steps shown below will help you make the most of the color range choosing tool.:

- ✦ Open the image you want to select from in Photoshop and use Ctrl/Cmd +A to select your entire image.
- ✦ From the **Menu Bar**, click on **Select.**

- ✦ In the **Select`s** drop-down menu, select **Color Range.**

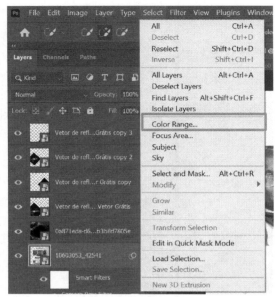

✦ The window changes. From the drop-down option,

○ **Select:** The Select option is located right at the top of the dialog box. It is set to Sampled Colors by default:

What we choose to select in the image is controlled by the Select option. When the option for Sampled Colors is selected, the Color Range command functions similarly to the Magic Wand.

When you click on the term "Sampled Colors," a list of the different selection options will show up so you may choose. For example, we can instantly choose all the pixels that are that color (reds, yellows, blues, etc.) by choosing a certain color from the list. Alternatively, we can select the Mid-tones to find the area of the image that lies between the brightest and darkest pixels, or Highlights or Shadows to rapidly identify the image's brightest or darkest pixels, respectively. You can choose colors that mimic popular skin tones with the Skin Tones feature. These additional options can be helpful in certain situations, so leave the option set to Sampled Colors, which is what we'll be concentrating on.

o **The Eye Dropper Tool**: We use an eyedropper tool to select the image with Color Range. In fact, Color Range provides us with three eyedropper tools: one for initial selection[ ], one for adding to the selection b[ ], and one for removing from the selection[ ]. These tools are located on the right side of the dialog box.

o **The Selection Preview Window**: We may observe a real-time preview of the region or areas of the image that we have selected using the eyedroppers in the selection preview window, which is situated at the bottom of the dialogue box. The preview box displays our selection as a greyscale image. Layer masks function precisely like the preview window does. The fully selected areas of the image will appear white in the preview window, while the unselected areas will appear black.

To display the selection in the image window, use the Selection Preview option.

None Displays the first picture.

Pixels that are not selected are displayed in **Black**, partially selected pixels are displayed in **Grey**, and fully selected pixels are displayed in **White**. For pixels that have been selected, Black Matte shows the original image; for pixels that have not, it displays black. Vibrant images complement this choice. When a white matte is used, unselected pixels show white, and chosen pixels show the original image. This option works well for dark photos. You can select a custom color in the Quick Mask Options dialogue box to replace the original image with unselected areas.

.

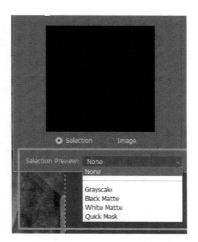

- o **Fuzziness**: Just like **Tolerance** works in the **Magic Wand Tool**, so does **Fuzziness** in **Color Range.** The selection's color range is controlled by the

Fuzziness parameter, which also affects how many pixels are partially picked (gray areas in the selection preview). To limit the color range, set a low Fuzziness value; to widen the range, set a high value.

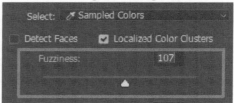

o **Detect Face**: This feature work with the skin tones option for accurate skin tone selection.

o **Localized Color Clusters & Range**: As soon as we turn on Localized Color Clusters, another option, Range, becomes available directly below the Fuzziness slider.

If you chose Localized Color Clusters, you may use the Range slider to change how close or how far a color must be from the sample points to be included in the selection. When Range is set to 100% (or the **Localized Color** Clusters option is disabled), Photoshop will look throughout the image for patches of matching color to add to our selection. But by shifting the slider to the left and reducing the Range value, we tell Photoshop to disregard areas of the image that are too far away and only focus on the areas that are close to where we clicked.

o **Invert**: This tool is located just below the eye dropper tool in the color range preview window. As the name implies, it is used to invert selections.

o After you`re done with making adjustments to your selections, then Click **Ok** to close out the Color Range preview window.

Focus Area

If we need to separate a person or subject from the background and that person or subject happens to be in focus (within the depth of field) while the background is blurred and out of focus, Photoshop can now analyze an image, identify what is in focus and what is not, and then select just the area we need. The Focus Area selection tools make this possible.

To use the Focus Area selection tool effectively, follow the procedure below:

- In the **Select** drop-down menu from the **Menu Bar**, Select **Focus Area.**
- The Focus Area window pops up,

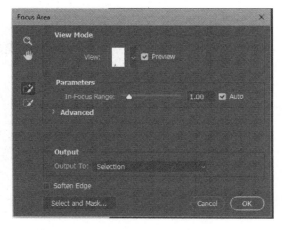

- Photoshop will look for in-focus elements and generate an extremely accurate Auto selection. Drag the In-Focus **Range slider** in the Parameters box to enlarge or reduce the selection. Experiment until you discover a solid foundational option.

156

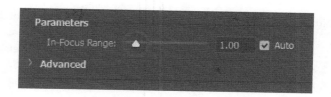

✦ Set the **View Mode** to your preference and note that the **Hand** and **Zoom tool** are options are available for quick access if you need them. The **Preview option** allows you to check the changes you have made to your image

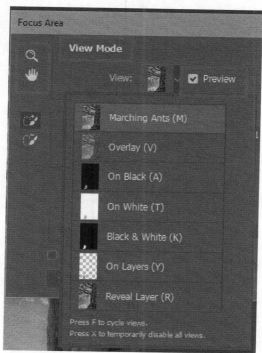

✦ The **Image Noise Level slider** is located in the **Advanced section**. To change the Focus Area's sensitivity to image noise, move the slider to the left or right.

◆ It's time to exercise additional manual control over the selection using two powerful brush tools, the **Focus Area Add Tool** and the **Focus Area Subtract Tool**, once you've made the most improvements to the original selection using the In-Focus Range slider (as well as the Image Noise Level slider). We can access them by clicking on their icons on the left side of the Focus Area dialogue box. The Focus Area Add Tool, which is the one at the top with the plus sign in the icon, is selected by default:

Quick Tip: On the keyboard, hitting the letter **E** will switch between the Focus Area Add and Focus Area Select tools.

◆ By choosing the **Soften Edges option** in the dialog box's lower left, you can smooth out the edges of your image.

◆ If you're satisfied with your choice so far, you may select from a variety of output kinds using the **Output To** option located near the bottom of the Focus Area dialog box. The list of choices is opened by clicking the output type box. We can create it as a new layer, a layer mask, or the conventional "marching ants" selection outline, among other output formats:

◆ Once you are done with making your selection, Click **Ok**

Using The Quick Mask Mode

The Quick Mask Mode is a very simple way of making selection in Photoshop.

To use the Quick Mask Mode follow the procedures below,

- ⬥ You can open the Quick Mask Mode either of the following ways;
  - ○ Click the icon found at the bottom of the toolbar.

  - ○ Additionally, you can open a Quick Mask by selecting **Select** > **Edit in Quick Mask** from the Select drop-down menu.

- On the Keyboard, click The **Q** key and it opens you up to the Quick Mask Mode automatically.
- The areas that are not selected while in this mode will be covered by a red color overlay, while the selected pixels will be left exposed.

Paint over with white Brush to add to the mask or black brush to deduct from it (your strokes will appear as a red overlay). Grayscale brush can also be used to create semi-transparent choices.

To change the mask's color and opacity, double click on it. Additionally, you have the option to have the mask display the selected regions rather than the unselected regions. To see marching ants encircling the selected area, click the **icon** or **Q** once more.

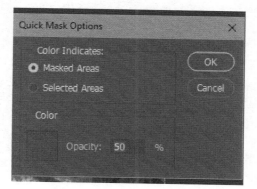

Selecting and Masking

The selection tools mentioned above are used to choose certain objects or regions of photographs, as their names imply. You can choose to change or remove your choices.

The simplest way to get rid of part of your selection without destroying the original image is to mask it.

As indicated earlier, you can use the selection tools to choose a piece of an image, but you can also use masking to isolate the selected region. Masking is a technique used to eliminate other parts of an image that aren't selected. However, any alterations made to an image using masking are not irreversible because it is unbreakable. You may easily reverse the changes you made by removing or disabling the layer mask. Because of the layer mask, masking is unbreakable.

The Select and Mask Options
In Photoshop, this function is also a selection option. You can choose and hide your choices with it. Advanced features that let you fine-tune your choices to your liking are integrated into this option. Other selection tools can also access the Select and Mask Window for additional image editing.

You can access the select and mask option either of the following ways,

- From the **Options Bar** of the **Object Selection tools**, **Quick Selection tools** and the **Lasso tools.**

- Ultimately, you can access the select and mask option from the **Select** drop-down menu from the **Menu bar.**

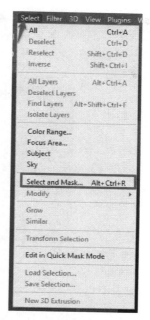

To use the Select and Mask option, follow the procedure below:

- ✦ After making your selection with any of the selection tools, access the selection and mask option from either of the following ways above.
- ✦ The select and mask option becomes enabled,

- o **Quick Selection Tool**: Don't be surprised that a quick selection tool is also available in the select and mask window, this tool functions like the typical quick selection tool.

163

When you click or click-drag the area you want to select, make a rapid selection based on similarity in color and texture. The Quick Selection tool automatically and logically produces a border, so the selection you make doesn't need to be exact.

- o **Refine Edge Brush Tool:** Use this tool to adjust the boundary region where edge refinement takes place precisely. For example, to add small details to the selection, brush over soft parts like hair or fur. To change the brush size, press the bracket keys.

- o **Brush Tool**: Use the Quick Selection tool (or another selection tool) to create a crude selection, and then use the Refine Edge Brush tool to make it more precise. Use the Brush tool to clean up or complete details now.

Use the Brush tool to fine-tune a selection, in either Add mode to paint over the region you want to pick or Subtract mode to paint over the area you don't want to select.

o **Object Selection Tool**: Around an object, draw a lasso or a rectangular area. The object is located and automatically selected using the Object Selection tool inside the specified zone.

o **Lasso Tool**: Make selection borders by hand. You can choose exactly what you want by using this tool.

165

o **Polygonal Lasso Tool**: Draw portions of a selection border with straight edges. You can use this tool to make precise or arbitrary selections. When you right-click the Lasso Tool, you can choose this tool from the available selections.

o **Hand Tool**: Navigate around an image document quickly. Drag this tool around the picture canvas after selecting it. Holding down the spacebar while using any other tool allows you to switch to the Hand tool swiftly.

o **Zoom Tool**: Magnify the image and move around it.

o **Option Bars**: The Options Bar carries the extra information of a tool. The image below is the options bar for the quick selection tool.

Other options available in the options bar are below,

  ✦ **Add** or **Subtract**: The refining area may be increased or decreased. Adjust the brush size if necessary.

  ✦ **Sample All Layers:** creates a selection based on all layers, as opposed to only the one that is currently selected.

- ⬍ **Select Subject:** Select the main subjects in a photo in a single click.
- ⬍ **Refine Hair:** Find and improve challenging hair selections with just one click. For the best outcomes, combine with Object Aware.

Refine the Selection

We continue to examine the Select and Mask Workspace in this section. You can adjust your selection in the Properties section of the Select and Mask workspace. To accomplish this, change the following settings:

- **View Mode**: Choose one of the following view modes for your selection from the View pop-up menu:

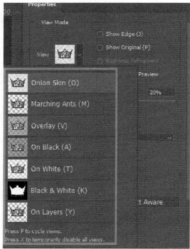

- o **Onion Skin (O)**: visualizes the choice as an animated onion skin scheme
- o **Marching Ants (M):** the selection's borders as marching ants.
- o **Overlay (V)**: visualizes the selection as a transparent color. Areas that are not selected are shown in that color. The standard shade is red.
- o **On Black (A)**: Place the selection over a black background when you pick this option.
- o **On White (T)**: positions the selected area against a white background.
- o **Black & White (K)**: Creates a black and white mask out of the selection.
- o **On Layers (Y):** surrounds the selection with areas of transparency.

Press **F** to switch between the modes, then **X** to turn off each option for a while.

- o **Show Edge**: Shows the area of refinement.

- Show original: Shows the original selection.

- High-Quality Preview: This produces a precise preview of the modification. This decision may affect performance. To view a higher-resolution preview, hold down the left mouse button (mouse down) while working with the image that has this option selected. Even with the mouse down, a lower-resolution preview appears when this option is deselected.

- Transparency/Opacity: Transparency and opacity are set for the View Mode.
- **Refine Modes**: Color Aware and object-aware modes are the two modes present in this setting section.
  - Color Aware: Choose this mode for simple or contrasting backgrounds.
  - Object Aware: Select this mode if the background has intricate hair or fur.

- **Edge Detection Settings**:
  - Radius: The size of the selection boundary where edge refinement occurs is determined by this parameter. Use a smaller radius for sharp edges and a greater radius for softer edges.

o **Smart Radius**: allows you to adjust the width of the refining zone that surrounds the edge of your selection. Among other things, this option is useful if the portrait you select contains both shoulders and hair. In these pictures, the hair might require more fine-tuning than the shoulders, which have a more consistent edge.

- **Global Refinement Settings**:
  o **Smooth**: Smoothens the selection border's rough edges (such as "hills and valleys") to give it a more even appearance.
  o **Feather**: Softens the boundary between the selected area and the pixels around it.
  o **Contrast**: Soft-edged transitions along the selection border become more abrupt as they are magnified. The Smart Radius option and refining tools are frequently more efficient.
  o **Shift Edge**: Shifts soft-edged borders inward when the value is negative or outward when the value is positive. It may be possible to get rid of undesirable backdrop colors from selection edges by moving these borders inward.

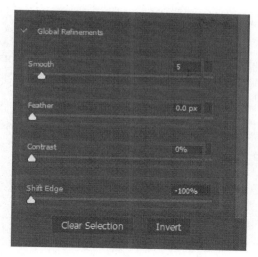

- **Output Settings:**
  - **Decontaminate Colors**: To decontaminate colors, this setting's option substitutes the color of nearby entirely selected pixels for color fringes. There is an inverse relationship between the degree of color replacement and the softness of the selection boundaries. Move the slider to change the level of decontamination. The maximum strength, 100%, is the default setting. Because it changes the color of the pixels, this option requires exporting to a new layer or document. Save the first layer so you may return to it if needed.
  - **Output To:** This indicates whether the result of the refined selection is a new layer, a new document, or a selection or mask on the current layer.

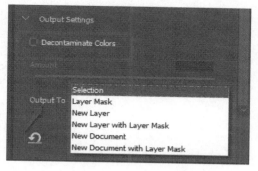

Additional information to take note:

⬦ To return the settings to the ones you saw when you first opened the Select and Mask workspace, click 🔄 (**Reset The Workspace**). Additionally, choosing this option restores the image's initial selections and masks from when you first opened the Select and Mask workspace.

To preserve the settings for use with subsequent photos, select **Remember Settings**. If the current image is opened again in the **Select and Mask workspace**, the settings are applied again to all ensuing photos.

CHAPTER SEVEN

TYPOGRAPHY; USING TEXTS IN PHOTOSHOP

What you will learn in this chapter.

- **The typeface varieties used in design.**
- **Photoshop text usage instructions.**
- **How to get proficient with the character panel's settings**.

Understanding Typography

The practice of arranging letters and text such that they are easy for readers to read, understand, and find visually appealing is known as typography.

Typeface look, style, and structure are all used to elicit particular feelings and deliver particular messages. In other words, typography makes the writing more lively.

The majority of the various typographic components can also be found in Photoshop's Character Panel.

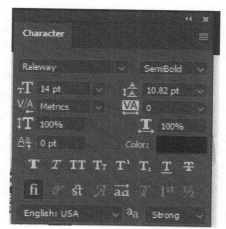

Some of the elements of typography are explained below. explained below;

- ⬥ **Fonts and Typeface**: A typeface is a design style that includes a range of characters in various sizes and weights, whereas a font is a graphic depiction of a text character.

  In essence, a typeface is a collection of connected fonts; by fonts, we mean the many weights, widths, and styles that comprise a typeface.

Three fundamental types of typefaces exist: The three basic types of typefaces are Serif, Sans-Serif, and Script.

- o **Serif**: A serif is a typeface with additional markings at the end of each letter. Because of these tiny strokes and elements, serif fonts convey a sense of tradition, history, authority, and integrity.

SERIF

- o **Sans-Serif**: As their name implies, sans-serif fonts are distinguished by what they lack. Because it doesn't have the more traditional serif strokes and dashes, the sans-serif font family is thought to be much bolder and more modern. It is therefore easier to read and, when utilized in headlines, it draws attention more successfully than serifs.

SANS SERIF

- o **Scripts**: As its name again suggests, the function of this typeface is more decorative than comprehensible. As a result, brand names, logos, and short titles use them far more often.

- ✦ **Color**: Color is one of typography's most intriguing features, and it's here that interface designers can truly show off their imagination and elevate their work. However, text color should not be taken lightly; when done correctly, it can highlight the text and convey the tone of the message. Value, hue, and saturation are the three primary components of color, and even for people who are blind or visually impaired, a clever designer can balance these components to produce writing that is both aesthetically pleasing and easy to read.

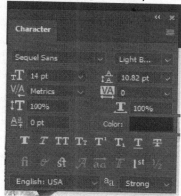

Designers usually assess this by looking at the text in greyscale, or without color, and adjusting it if it contrasts too brightly or too darkly with the background color.

- **Font Size**: The function of the text in the design dictates the size of any typeface you use. By allocating the size of your sentences to their relative importance, you can establish the hierarchy in a design.

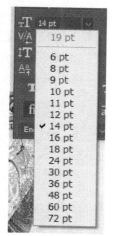

- **Leading**: Leading is the space between lines of text.

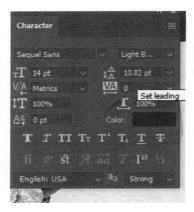

✦ **Kerning**: Kerning is the technique of varying the spacing between individual characters.

Kerning attempts to balance the appearance of whitespace between characters to provide a more uniformly dispersed type. This is important to keep in mind when utilizing large headers and fonts. Although kerning is less important in paragraphs with small types, it can be quite helpful when trying to minimize line breaks in your design.

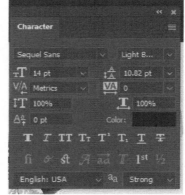

✦ **Whitespace**: The empty area in a composition is known as white space or negative space.

Your text will be challenging to read if your font and other design components are crowded and placed too closely together. Whitespace is useful in this situation.

✦ **Hierarchy**: Hierarchy is among the most crucial typographic rules. The goal of typographic hierarchy is to create a clear division between regular text and important content that should be read and noticed first.

Using Texts in Photoshop

You can add text to your file by using the Type tool. You can use it for many different purposes, such as adding text to photos to create an invitation, holiday card, or poster. Furthermore, you can alter the text to meet your needs.

The Toolbar contains the Type tool. Other type tool variations, such as the **Horizontal Type Tool, Vertical Type Tool, Horizontal Type Mask Tool,** and **Vertical Type Mask Tool,** are nestled inside the type tools.

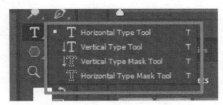

- ✦ **The horizontal type tool** is your standard typing instrument. You may make simple text on a horizontal plane using it.
- ✦ You can generate basic text that is created on a vertical plane using **the Vertical Type Tool** (from top to bottom).
- ✦ **Horizontal Type Mask Tool** - Rather than displaying live text, this tool generates a selection of the text. Following that, the selections can be utilized to make masks and clips.
- ✦ Instead of displaying live text, **the vertical type mask tool** generates a selection of the text. A vertical plane will be used to format the text. Following that, the selections can be utilized to make masks and clips.

The Character Panel and The Paragraph panel

In Photoshop, the **Paragraph Panel, Character Panel,** or **Options Bar** are used for text editing and type manipulation. These two tools have the advantage of giving you more options than the Options Bar. Effective use of the type tool depends on these two panels. While the Paragraph Panel shows your type's alignment options, the Character Panel shows all the options you need to modify your type efficiently. The Paragraph Palette is quite useful when working with paragraphs or lengthy text passages. The Paragraph panel has options for word hyphenation, indentation, and alignment.

The Options Bar

The Character Panel

The Paragraph Panel

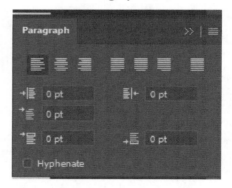

The options below are made available by either of the three panels above are;

✦ **Font Family**: You can choose from any font on your computer. If the font you wish to use isn't currently installed on your computer, you can add it using the Add Fonts dialogue box. Both the Character panel and the Options bar include this option.

❖ **Font Style**: You can choose between bold, bold italic, italic, and regular. Both the Character panel and the Options bar include this option.

❖ **Font Size**: A selection of preset sizes or a numerical value can be entered. Both the Character panel and the Options bar include this option.

- **Leading**: This is the separation between lines of text. You can enter a numeric value or choose from a range of pre-set figures.

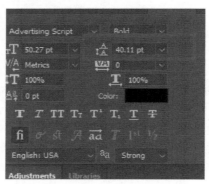

- **Tracking**: This setting determines the amount of space between each character in a text passage.

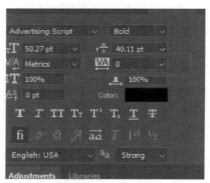

- **Kerning**: The kerning controls the distance between two specific letters or characters. Despite their apparent similarities, kerning and tracking are sometimes mistaken with one another. Kerning controls the distance between two specific characters, whereas tracking establishes the distance between a range of characters.

✦ **Vertical and Horizontal Scale**: Behind the Kerning and Tracking choices in the Character panel are the Vertical Scale (left) and Horizontal Scale (right) settings. These settings allow you to scale the type either vertically or horizontally.

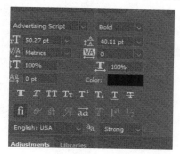

✦ **Baseline Shift**: When you move characters above or below the baseline, this is the distance between them.

✦ **Anti-aliasing**: Anti-aliasing is used to preserve the appearance of smooth text edges. In the absence of anti-aliasing, most letters would have jagged, blocky edges. Both the Character panel and the Options bar include this option.

181

♦ **Text Color**: Click the color swatch to select any color from the Color Picker. You may also create "tints" by choosing a color and then specifying how light or dark you want it to be. Tints work especially well for creating subtle color variations, such as many shades of grey. Both the Character panel and the Options bar include this option.

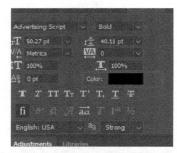

♦ **Faux Bold**: This option allows you to bolden a type when the font you are using does not include them.

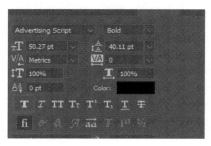

♦ **Faux italic**. This option allows you to apply the italics effect to your texts.

✦ **All Caps**: This option converts all your texts into uppercase letters when checked.

✦ **Small Caps**: This allows you to convert all your texts into lowercase letters

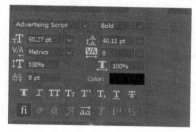

✦ **Superscript and Subscript**: Superscript and subscript text (sometimes called superior and inferior text) are reduced-size text that is elevated or lowered proportionately to a typeface's baseline.

✦ **Underline and Strikethrough**: The Underline option allows you to underline a text while Strikethrough creates a line that cuts through your selected texts.

✦ **Language Selection**: The Character panel's lower left corner contains the Language Selection box. Although it would be fantastic if Photoshop could translate our content between languages, this feature isn't meant to achieve that. Just make sure you're using the correct hyphenation and spelling for the language you've chosen.

The Options below are available in the Paragraph Panel.

✦ **The Alignment Options**: At the top of the paragraph panel is a row of icons for aligning and justifying our content. The first three symbols in the row on the left stand for the alignment options. The order in which they appear is **Left Align Text**, **Centre Text**, and **Right Align Text**. The only paragraph alternatives available in the alternatives Bar are these three alignment choices.

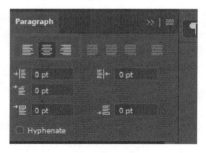

✦ **The Justification Options**: The following four icons in the row at the top of the paragraph panel are the justification options. From left to right, the following are listed: **Justify Last Left**, **Justify Last Centered**, **Justify Last Right**, and finally, **Justify All**. Only the Paragraph panel has these options. Going ahead, we will only examine the options through the Paragraph panel. Both here and in the Options Bar, you can only choose from the alignment options we just reviewed above.

Photoshop adjusts the word spacing based on any of these justification settings so that each line of text in the paragraph fills the text box's width from left to right, creating a "block" of text. The way Photoshop handles the final line of the paragraph is the only difference between the four options.

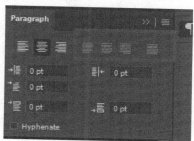

✦ **The Indent options**: Three indent options are available underneath the alignment and justification icons: **Indent Left Margin (top left)**, **Indent Right Margin (top right)**, and **Indent First Line (bottom left)**. By default, all three are set to 0 points:

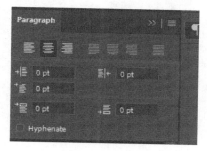

These options allow us to insert a space between the entire paragraph and either the text box's left or right sides or just the first line. To modify the settings of any of the indent options, you can either click inside the input box and manually type a value.

✦ **Paragraph Spacing Options**: The suitably called **Add Space Before Paragraph** (left) and **Add Space After Paragraph** (right) tools in Photoshop allow us to add space before or after a paragraph.

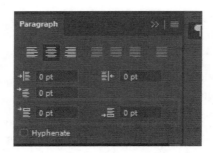

✦ **Hyphenate**: Hyphenation is a particularly helpful tool when using any of the justification options since it allows Photoshop to divide longer sentences into separate lines, which makes it easier to arrange the text in a more visually appealing manner. If you dislike hyphenation or simply don't want to use it in a certain situation, you may easily uncheck the option to prevent it.

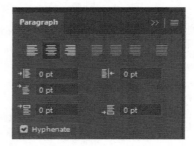

Other commands and more advanced features can be found in the Type Menu located at the Menu bar.

Working With Texts

To insert texts in a file,

➕ Get your file open in Photoshop.

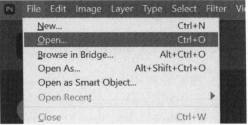

➕ Click 'T' to select the Type tool immediately, or select it from the toolbar. The tool that lets you add text horizontally is chosen by default.

➕ To view the various type tool variations, left-click the Type tool.

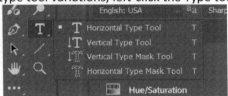

➕ Do you want to add a title or a heading? Click anywhere on the canvas to type it. This is known as point text in Photoshop, or you may insert your text by dragging the mouse pointer to create a bounding box. When you want to type a paragraph, you use this.

➕ The T icon in the Layers panel indicates that a type layer has been created automatically when you generate point or paragraph text.

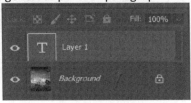

- The **Options Bar**, **Character Panel**, and Paragraph Panel **are** where you can change your font settings.
- Enter your text. To save your changes, click the settings button or press **Esc**. Then you can proceed.

To Select Text(s),

- Launch the Photoshop file containing the text you wish to edit. To enable editing, make sure the text you wish to change is on a type layer.
- To select the entire text or paragraph on a type layer, double-click the text you want to pick after selecting the **Move tool** (⊕) from the toolbar.
- To choose one or more characters on a type layer, just select the **Type tool** from the **toolbar**, click, and then move the mouse pointer over the characters you want to pick.

To edit text(s),

- To make the desired text changes, open the Photoshop document. Make sure the text you want to update is on a type layer so that editing may take place.
- Select the **Type tool** from the toolbar.
- Select the content that needs editing.
- Using the **Character Panel** or the **Options bar** at the top, you can alter the font type, font size, font color, text alignment, and text style.
- Click on the options bar at the end to save your changes.

To Copy and Paste Text(s),

It's crucial to understand that you can copy and paste text from other documents into your Photoshop project (PSD) before starting this exercise. from a web page, Word document, PDF, or another Photoshop file, for example (PSD).

- To copy and paste from a non-photoshop file do the following,
    - To pick text in a non-Photoshop document, such as a Word document, PDF, or web page, simply click and drag the pointer over the text.
    - To copy the highlighted text, hit **Control+C** on a Windows computer or **Command+C** on a Mac.
    - Select the Type tool from the toolbar, then open the Photoshop document (PSD) where you wish to paste the copied text.
    - From the Layers panel, choose the type layer that you wish to paste the text into. If you don't have a type layer, you can create a new one.
    - To paste your text, select **Edit > Paste** or hit **Command+V** on a Mac or **Control+V** on a Windows computer. Select **Edit > Undo Paste Text** to undo.

- ❖ To copy and paste from another Photoshop document
  - o To copy the text from a PSD, open the PSD.
  - o Choose **Edit** > **Copy** after selecting the text you wish to copy, or you may just click **Command+C** (on Mac OS) or **Control+C** (on Windows).
  - o Select a type layer in the PSD after opening it and pasting the text within. If you wish to add another type layer or don't have any type layers, you can simply do so by creating a new type layer.
  - o To paste your text in the center of your canvas, select **Edit** > **Paste**. To paste the text exactly as it appeared in the PSD that you had copied, select **Edit** > **Paste Special** > **Paste in Place**.

To resize text(s),

- ❖ Open the Photoshop document that contains the desired text changes. To allow for editing, make sure the text you wish to change is on a type layer.
- ❖ Select the image you desire to resize and do either of the following;
  - o Change the size of the texts in the **Character panel**.

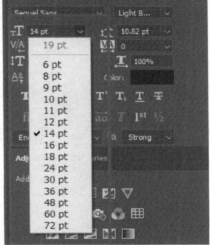

  - o Change the size of the texts in the **Options bar**

  - o Select on the type layer you desire to resize and click on the bounding box to resize it. Ensure that Show Transform Controls in checked in the **Options Bar**

- ✦ To save your adjustments, click ☑ in the options bar at the end.

To resize one or more characters on a type layer,

- ✦ Open the Photoshop document that contains the text you desire to make changes to. To allow for editing, make sure the text you wish to change is on a type layer.
- ✦ Select the type layer you want to make changes to and do either of the following;
  - ○ Choose the 🔠font size option you desire in the **options bar**'s box or in the **Character Panel**. Real-time modifications are shown.
- ✦ You're finished after you click ☑ in the options bar! In the options bar, click ◌ to undo your changes.

To move text(s),

- ✦ The Photoshop document with the text you want to modify should be opened. Make sure the text you want to update is on a type layer so that editing is possible.
- ✦ The text you want to transfer is on a type layer; choose that layer.
- ✦ In the **toolbar**, pick the **Move tool**.
- ✦ Select **Auto Select Layer** in the options bar, and then click the text you want to transfer.

- ✦ The black arrow will then allow you to see the transform box.
- ✦ To position the text where you desire, click and drag the transform box, then let go of it.

To change Color pf Text(s),

- ✦ The Photoshop document with the text you want to modify should be opened. Make sure the text you want to update is on a type layer so that editing is possible.
- ✦ Click the text whose color you want to change, then choose the **Type tool** from the **toolbar**. The type layer's whole text is selected.
- ✦ In the **Options bar** or in the **Character Panel**, select the **Color Picker (Text Color) icon.**

190

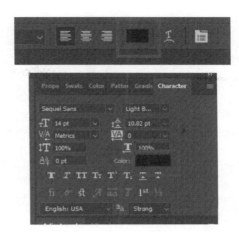

- Choose your color by adjusting the color slider as desired. As you choose several colors, you can instantly observe how your text color changes.
- Click **OK** after you're satisfied with the color of your text.

To align and justify Text(s),

- Open the Photoshop document containing the text you wish to edit. To allow for editing, ensure that the text you wish to change is on a type layer.
- From the Layers panel, choose the type layer that contains the paragraph you wish to justify.
- You may view the numerous Justify choices in the **Paragraph panel**. To see the changes as they happen, choose a choice.

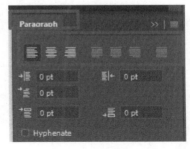

- Once you've chosen Justify, simply click ☑ in the choices menu to complete the process.

To rotate text(s)

- The text in the Photoshop document that you want to alter should be opened. Make sure the text you want to edit is on a type layer to enable editing.
- A type layer contains the text you wish to transfer; pick that layer.
- Select the **Move tool** from the **toolbar**.
- Click the text you want to transfer, then check **Auto Select Layer** and **Show Transform Controls** from the **Options bar**.
- Select the text by clicking it. The transform box surrounding your text will then be visible.
- Hover close to the transform box's corners. The cursor transforms into a double-headed arrow.
- To rotate the text in the desired direction, click and drag the curved arrow. In order to obtain a more precise rotation, you can also enter values in the options bar.
- You're finished after you click ☑ in the options bar!

CHAPTER EIGHT

TRANSFORMING IMAGES IN PHOTOSHOP

Understanding The Transform Tool in Photoshop

The morph tools in Photoshop are one feature that makes a user's work more efficient. The transform tool in Photoshop program enables us to alter the selected image in several ways, including scaling, rotating, and flipping. This chapter will explain how to use the program's transform tool and how to control the numerous parameters of this Photoshop feature. So let's start discussing this topic. Ctrl/Cmd + T is the keyboard shortcut for Photoshop's transformation tools.

Once you've accessed the morph function, you can either hold down the Ctrl/Cmd, Alt/Opt, or Shift keys separately or simultaneously to access further transform options, or you can left-click your mouse to open additional transform options. Photoshop has two main types of transform tools: Free Transform and Transform. We make a lot of things that aren't necessarily the exact size, rotation, or skew we want. We might alter or change anything by using the Transform and Free Transform Tools.

While the **Free Transform** function enables you to make multiple transformations at once, rather than one at a time, the **Transform** feature allows users to alter their object or selection in a variety of ways, such as scaling, rotating, distorting, and flipping (mirror).

Other transform Options in Photoshop
Photoshop's Free Transform and Transform buttons provide access to additional transform possibilities. The only difference between these two programs is how they conduct their operations. In this section, we'll examine the extra transform choices available in Photoshop's Transform tool.

193

- **Scale**: Free Transform's default action is to scale images. The image will therefore scale according to the handle you move. To scale your items proportionately in Photoshop, hold down the **Shift key**. You can scale an object to make it larger or smaller. To scale an image proportionately from the center, hold down the **Alt/Opt** key.
- **Rotate**: You can move your objects either clockwise or anticlockwise with this Transform option. This functionality can be used by either navigating via the Transform options or by moving the mouse pointer outside the Free Transform box, which will rotate it into a curving, double-sided arrow.

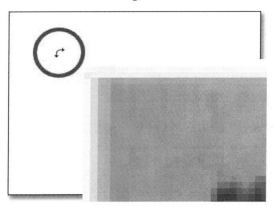

Use the Shift Key to constrain the rotation to 15-degree increments.

- **Skew**: Skewing is just the result of an image not being straight. Skew allows you to move a corner point alone or in tandem with the one on the opposite side by depressing the Option (Alt) Key. With Skew chosen, click on the top or bottom handle and drag to skew the image to the left or right.

- **Distort**: If an artist wishes to change the wallpaper in a room or replace a picture on a wall, this is a great solution because of how accurately objects may be deformed to fit into designated spaces. You can use distortion to adjust the edge as you want or to pick up corner points for exact individual movement.
- **Perspective**: To produce a mathematical perspective, perspective corrects an object's distortion. Shifting the center edge point causes the item to warp from side to side. Adjusting a corner point causes both corners to move inward or outward, depending on whether the Transform Box is being reduced or expanded.
- **Warp:** Clicking the Warp icon opens a grid that can be adjusted to produce different distortions within the Transforming command. If the edges of a panoramic don't quite line up, this option can be quite helpful.

Other transform options are:

- Rotate 180°
- Rotate 90° Clockwise
- Rotate 90° Counter Clockwise
- Flip Horizontal
- Flip Vertical

The aforementioned options are self-explanatory and frequently utilized in photo editing to quickly alter shapes.

Free Transform
You can do multiple transformations simultaneously with the Free Transform command, such as rotation, scale, skew, distortion, and perspective. An alternative is a warp transformation. Instead of choosing different commands, you just hold down a key on your keyboard to switch between transformation types.

To make the most of the Free Transform, adhere to the steps listed below.

- Select the object you want to transform
- Do one of the following to carry out the transform operation;
  - Select the **Free Transform** under **Edit** in the **Menu Bar** (upper-side of Photoshop's workspace)

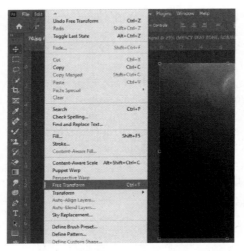

o Select the **Move tool** () to change a selection, pixel-based layer, or **selection boundary**. Then, in the settings menu, choose **Show Transform Controls**.

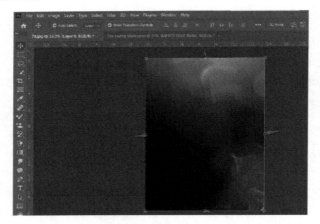

o Choose the **Path Selection tool** () to transform a vector shape or path. Then, in the settings menu, choose **Show Transform Controls**.

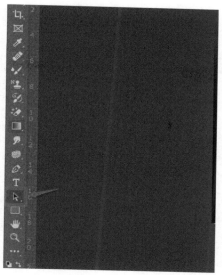

- ♦ Do one or more of the following:
    - ○ To scale by dragging, do one of the following:
        - ▪ Drag a corner handle to proportionately scale the layer if the Maintain Aspect Ratio button (Link icon) is selected in the Options

          bar.
        - ▪ Drag a corner handle to scale the layer irregularly if the Options bar's Maintain Aspect Ratio button (Link icon) is deactivated.

        - ▪ When transforming, keep holding down the Shift key to switch between proportional and non-proportional scaling behavior.
    - ○ Enter percentages in the Width and Height text boxes in the options bar to scale numerically. To keep the aspect ratio, click the Link button.

    - ○ Move the cursor outside the bounding border so that it forms a curved, two-sided arrow, and then drag to **rotate**. To limit the rotation to 15° increments, press **Shift**.

197

- Enter degrees in the rotation text box in the options bar to rotate numerically. ![rotation box]

- Holding down the Alt or Option key while dragging a handle will distort to be relative to the center point of the enclosing border.

- Press Ctrl (Windows) or Command (Mac OS) and drag a handle to freely **distort**.

- Press Ctrl+Shift on a Windows or Mac computer to **skew**, then drag a side handle. The pointer transforms into a white arrowhead with a tiny double arrow when it is placed over a side handle.

- Enter degrees in the H (horizontal skew) and V (vertical skew) text boxes in ![skew box] the options bar to **skew** numerically.

- To apply perspective, press Ctrl+Alt+Shift (Windows) or Command+Option+Shift (Mac OS) and drag a corner handle. When the pointer is over a corner handle, it turns into a grey arrowhead.

- Click the 🏛 button labeled Switch Between Free Transform and Warp Modes in the settings box to warp. To change an item's shape, drag control points, or select a warp style from the Warp pop-up menu in the options bar. The shape of the warp can be modified with the square handle after selecting it from the Warp pop-up menu. ![warp button]

- Click a square on the reference point locator in the options bar to change the reference point. ⚏

- The X (horizontal position) and Y (vertical position) text boxes in the options bar must have values for the new location of the reference in order to move an item. To set the new position in relation to the present position, click the Relative Positioning button.

✦ Once your transformation is complete and you're ready to save your changes, double-click anywhere inside the transformation marquee, click the Commit button in the options bar, or press Return on a Mac or Windows computer.

![commit cancel buttons]

✦ Press Esc or click the Cancel button in the options bar to stop the transformation.

198

Transform

Using the Transform tool, users can alter their object or selection in a variety of ways, such as scaling, rotating, distorting, and flipping (mirror).

- ↕ Select a layer or make a new selection to use the transform function.
- ↕ Select **Transform** from the **Edit menu**, then choose the type of transformation you want to apply.

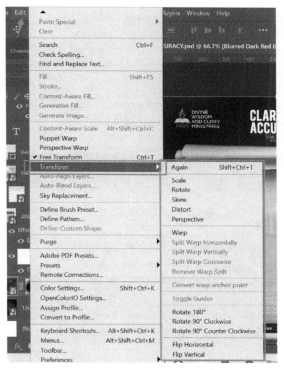

- ↕ Your selection will be surrounded by a bounding box that you can manipulate using the handles. Your image will automatically change if you choose Rotate 180°, Rotate 90°, Flip Horizontal, or Flip Vertical.

Content-Aware: Generative Fill, Content-Aware Fill, and Content-Aware Scale

Each of these Photoshop features is more sophisticated than the others, but they are all related. They are also employed to address various issues. Although their methods of operation differ, they all employ the Color algorithm to do their tasks. The **AI Generative Fill**, **Content-Aware Fill**, and **Content-Aware Scale** will all be covered in this section. The following chapter on retouching tools will cover other content-aware tools, such as the Content-Aware Move tool.

Using AI Generative Fill

This new function is part of every new Photoshop release. In contrast to other content-aware tools, Adobe Photoshop's Generative Fill function allows you to add and remove material with simple text prompts powered by Adobe Firefly generative AI. The contextual bar provides access to the Generative Fill. Generative Fill is used for three primary purposes:

- ✛ To and remove replace objects in images.
- ✛ For Generative Fill Outcrop.
- ✛ For Generative Expand.

If you can't seem to find your contextual task bar, do the following to enable it.

- ✛ Select **Window** from the **Menu Bar**.

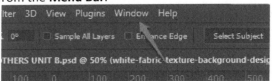

- ✛ Scroll down and select **Contextual Taskbar** to enable it.

To effectively perform texts to image with the generative fill, do the following.

- ✛ Select the portion you want to remove and replace with any of the selection tools.

- On the Contextual Taskbar, pick **Generative Fill**. Then, type the description you want, and the region you've chosen will automatically fill it in (make sure you have an internet connection).
  Options for your generated images will be made available in the **Properties Panel**.

To perform a generative fit outcrop, do the following.

- Open the image on Photoshop and select the **Crop Tool** from the **Menu Bar**.

- Expand the Canvas around the image beyond the size of the image.

✦ Select **Generative Expand** on the contextual taskbar and click on **Generate** and the empty canvas will automatically fill itself up.

To perform a generative expand, do the following.

✦ Open the image on Photoshop and select the **Crop Tool** from the **Menu Bar**.

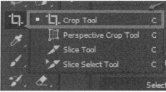

✦ Make your expansion with the **Crop tool**.

- Select **Generative Expand** in the **Option Settings**.

- Then, select **Generate** in the contextual taskbar.

Content-Aware Fill

Photoshop's Content-Aware feature allows you to do subtle photo edits. The Content-Aware tool in Photoshop looks at the pixels that are close by and guess what the missing pixels might be. This makes it easy to remove objects from photos without leaving any evidence behind.

Use the content-aware fill by following the guidelines listed below;

- Simply use the lasso tool to pick the item you wish to remove.

✦ After creating your selection, use either of the following methods
   o Go to **Edit** > **Fill**

   o Left-click your mouse and a window pops up, Select **the Content-Aware Fill** for direct result or Select **Fill.**

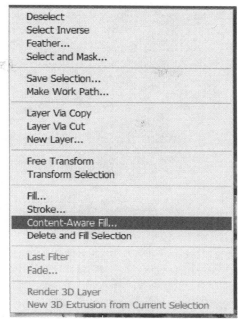

✦ After selecting **Fill**, A window pops up, From the **Contents** drop-down menu, select **Content-Aware.**

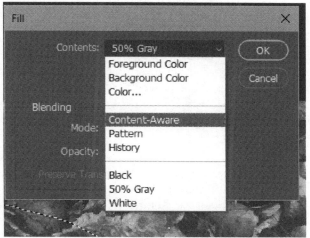

✦ Click **Ok** after you are done adjusting your settings (making adjustments to the settings are not always necessary)

✦ Now, leave the Content-Aware to perform its magic.

Content-Aware Scale

The content-aware scaling tool allows us to change an image's size without compromising the important elements of the picture. Using the Content-Aware Scale when resizing an image maintains all of its key visual components, including people, objects, animals, and so on. Unlike normal scaling, which uniformly affects all pixels when resizing an image, content-aware scaling mostly impacts pixels in areas with little visual information. Content-Aware Scale allows you to upscale or downscale images to improve composition, fit a layout, or change orientation. If you would like to apply some conventional scaling when resizing your image, you can choose to select a ratio of content-aware scaling to standard scaling.

You can use an alpha channel to protect specific areas of a picture when resizing it using the Content-Aware Scale. Content-aware scaling works on selections and layers. All bit depths and color modes, including RGB, CMYK, Lab, and greyscale, can be used to create images. Content-aware scaling does not work with adjustment layers, layer masks, individual channels, Smart Objects, 3D layers, video layers, multiple layers operating simultaneously, or layer groups.

Use the content-aware scale efficiently by following the steps listed below;

- Select the image you desire to scale
- From the **Edit Menu** in the **Menu bar**, Select **Content-Aware Scale**

- Choose one of the options listed below in the options bar:
  - **Location of Reference Point**: To choose the fixed point that the image will be resized around, click a square (⊞) on the reference point finder. By default, the image's focal point is in the middle.
  - **Use a Reference Point in Relative Positioning**: To specify the reference point's new location about its existing location, click the button.
  - **Point of Reference Position**: This option places the reference point in that precise spot. Enter the pixel dimensions for the X- and Y-axes.
  - **Scaling percentage**: provides an estimate of the image scaling in terms of the original size. Put a percentage in for the height (H) and width (W) (H). Click Maintain Aspect Ratio (⫶) if desired.
  - **Amount**: indicates the ratio of standard scaling to content-awareness. You can input a percentage for content-aware scaling by either typing in the text box or clicking the arrow and dragging the slider.
  - **Protect**: Select an alpha channel that designates the protected area.
  - **Protect skin tones**: This option tries to protect areas that have skin tones.

- To scale the image, drag a handle on the bounding box. Drag a corner handle while holding down Shift to scale accordingly. The pointer turns into a double arrow when it is over a handle.
- Either select Commit Transform (⊘) or Cancel Transform (✔).

207

How to protect an object while using the content-aware scale
- Make a selection around the content you want to be protected, and then navigate to the **Select Menu** and select **Save Selection**.
- After saving your selection, you can then proceed to scaling the entire image.
- Select **Content-Aware Scale** under **Edit**.
- Select the produced alpha channel from the options bar.

- To scale the image, move a handle along the bounding border.

The Crop Tool and its other related tools

In addition to being a tool, the crop tool contains three more tools. These are the **Slice Tool**, the **Perspective Crop Tool**, and the **Slice Select Tool**. Each of these tools will be examined in this section.

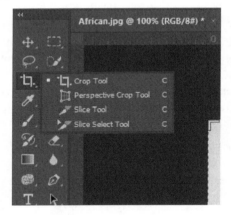

The Crop Tool

The process of cropping a photo involves removing certain components to enhance the composition or sharpen the focus. Use the Crop tool in Photoshop to crop and align photos. You can choose to preserve the pixels you've cropped in order to fine-tune the crop limits later on, and the crop tool is non-destructive. When cropping, the Crop tool provides easy methods for aligning an image.

You can choose a portion of an image and remove everything outside of it with the Crop tool (). The tool is located third from the top on the left side of the Photoshop Toolbox.

Although cropping reduces the size of an image, it is not the same as scaling. Unlike resizing, which makes the entire image and everything in it smaller or larger, cropping makes no changes to the size of the image's content.

Follow the procedures below to use the crop tool effectively.

- ✦ Launch Photoshop and open your picture.
- ✦ From the toolbar, select the Crop Tool. Crop borders are visible around the boundaries of the image.
- ✦ Either change the corner and edge handles or draw a new cropping region to specify the image's crop limitations.
- ✦ If required, modify the crop parameters in the **Options bar**.

- o **Size and Proportion**: Choose a crop box size or ratio. Furthermore, you have the choice to choose, input, or even create your own preset values for later use.

- o **Overlay Options**: To display cropping overlay guides, select a view. Other guidelines include the **Golden Ratio**, the **Rule of Thirds**, and the **Grid**. To cycle through each choice, press O.

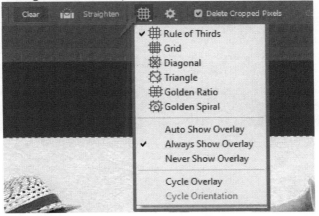

- ○ **Crop Options**: You can specify additional crop choices by selecting the settings (tool) menu.

  - ▪ **Use Classic mode**: If you want to use the Crop tool as it was in older versions of Photoshop, turn on this setting (CS5 and earlier).
  - ▪ **Auto Center Preview**: To center the preview on the canvas, turn on this setting
  - ▪ **Show Cropped Area**: To display the cropped area, turn on this option. Only the last area is previewed when this option is deactivated.
  - ▪ **Enable Crop Shield**: To add a hue to the sections that were cropped, use the crop shield. You can choose an opacity and color. When you alter the crop boundaries, the opacity is increased if you enable auto-adjust opacity
- ○ **Delete Cropped Pixels**: Disable this option to apply a non-destructive crop and maintain pixels outside the crop limitations. Non-destructive cropping preserves all pixels. Click the image afterward to see areas outside the current crop borders.
  This setting allows you to remove pixels that are outside the crop region. These pixels are gone and cannot be retrieved for later changes.

- ○ **Content-Aware**: Photoshop now intelligently fills in the blanks when you use the Crop tool to resize your canvas, rotate an image, or straighten it using content-aware technology.

- ✦ To crop the image, press Enter on a Windows computer or Return on a Mac.

Perspective Crop Tool

The second tool nestled within the crop tool is the perspective crop tool. While working on an image, you can adjust the perspective with the perspective crop tool. You can use the Perspective Crop tool to crop an image while altering the viewpoint. Use the perspective crop tool when working with photographs that have keystone distortion. Keystone distortion occurs when an item is taken at an angle rather than directly on. The edges of a tall building, for example, seem closer to one another at the top than they do at the bottom when photographed from the ground up.

Follow the procedure below to use the perspective crop tool effectively.

- ✦ Open the image you desire to crop in Photoshop
- ✦ Select the image in the layer panel
- ✦ Select the **Perspective Crop Tool** from the **Crop Tool** in the **Toolbar**

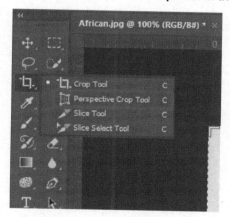

- ✦ Draw a marquee around the misaligned object. Compare the marquee's edges to the object's rectangular edges.

✦ To finish the perspective crop, hit Enter (Windows) or Return (Mac OS).

The Slice Tool
An entire Photoshop document can be divided into as many slices as needed with the Slice Tool. The slice tool divides the entire Photoshop document into many segments. Users can use it to break up a large image or piece of art into smaller pieces that fit together like jigsaw puzzles but with straight edges. Instead of cutting or cropping the image, the slice tool helps you extract a section of it. It can be used in many different contexts when a single large image needs to be broken up into several smaller ones. The diagram or picture can be separated into rectangular or square sections.

The crop tool portion of the tool menu in Photoshop includes a slice tool.

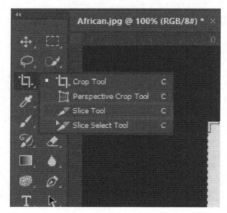

To use the Slice tool effectively, follow the procedures below.

✦ Launch your image in Photoshop
✦ Select the **Slice Tool** from the **Crop Tool** nest in the **Toolbar**.
✦ Adjust the settings of the tool in the **Options bar** (if Necessary)

- ○ **Style**: Three options exist for style: Normal, Fixed Aspect Ratio, and Fixed Size.

  - ▪ **Normal**: This choice is already chosen. It produces regular slices of any size and aspect ratio.
  - ▪ **Fixed aspect** ratio: The choices under this option are made by a fixed aspect ratio (i.e. width to height ratio). The width and height values are movable. Assume that the dimensions are 2 and 3. It will always produce slices with a width: height ratio of 2:3.
  - ▪ **Fixed Size**: With this choice, we can specify the slice's height and breadth in pixels.
- ○ **Height & Width**: When the style option is fixed aspect ratio or fixed size, these options are used to set the height and width of the selection.
- ○ **Slice from Guides**: With the aid of the rulers' guidance, we can also cut slices.
- ✥ Now, trim a section of the picture where you want it. You'll notice that Photoshop automatically generates further slices to match the remainder of the document after the initial slice is generated.
- ✥ After making your slices, Go to the **File menu** after making and choose the option to **save for the web** in the **Export** Section.

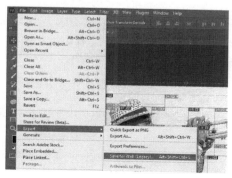

213

- A dialogue box appears on the screen, use the Shift key to select each of the slices that you have created.
- Go to the **Preset Option** and select the format that you want to save your slices in.

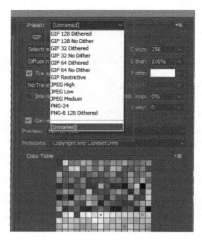

- A dialog box with the option to preserve the default settings comes on the screen after you click the **Save** button. In the dialog box, select **Save** to finally save your work.

The Select Slice Tool

The Slice Select Tool's main function is to help choose a certain slice. It has many capabilities, such as the ability to scale, move, and arrange slices on slides, making it a very useful and efficient tool for managing slices. The slice select tool is situated beneath the slice tool in the options menu.

To make good use of the Select Slice Tool, follow the steps listed below.

- Open your image in Photoshop
- After creating slices from your image, you need the Select Slice Tool to select each slice. So select the **Select slice tool** from the **Crop Tool** nest in the **Toolbar**.

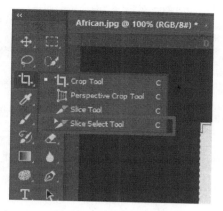

- It is now possible to move the slice and change its size. When using the slice choice tool, you can move the slice both horizontally and vertically in a straight line by holding down the SHIFT key.
- Adjust the tool`s settings on the **Options Bar**, if necessary.

- o **Ordering**: There are four ways to order a certain slice, and they are as follows:

  Starting from the left, we have:

  - **Bring to front**: Using this choice, the slice is brought to the front.
  - **Bring to forward**: This choice is used to incrementally bring the slice to the top. If there are two slices above the current slice, clicking this option once will move the slice to position two, and clicking it again will move it to the top (i.e. number one).
  - **Bring downward**: In the same manner as the preceding choice, but in the reverse order, this option is used to bring the slice to the bottom in steps.
  - **Bring to bottom**: By selecting this option, the slice is brought to the bottom.

- o **Promote**: By selecting this option, a user-defined slice is created from an automatic slice. The issue of how to determine if it is a user slice or an auto slice may now arise. The explanation is that auto slices do not have a scaling option enabled, while human slices can be modified using the slice choice tool.

o **Divide**: The user can split the selected slice into several smaller slices by selecting   this   option. When you choose the Divide option, a dialogue window like the one below will show :

As you can see, the dialog box is divided into two parts:

- **Horizontal Slice**: When selected, this option creates horizontal slices out of the slice.
- **Vertical Slice**: When selected, this option creates vertical slices out of the slice.

The following choices are now available in both sections:

- **Slices down, evenly spaced**: The user-specified number of evenly spaced slices is what this option does.
- **Pixels per slice**: The user-specified number of pixels is used to determine how many slices are made.

o **Align**: There are many alignment options for two or more selected slices. The question of how to select several slices may now be raised. To choose multiple levels with the slice select tool, you have to hold down the SHIFT key.

The aligned options are listed below:

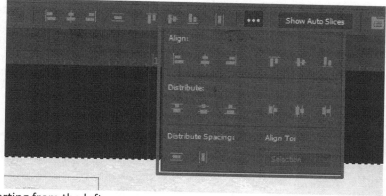

Starting from the left,

- **Align left edges**: The left edges of the chosen slice are aligned using this option.
- **Align center**: This choice is used to center the slices.
- **Align right edges**: Using this option, the right edges of the chosen slice are aligned.
- **Vertically Distribute**: This option is used to vertically distribute the layers that have been chosen.
- **Align top edges**: Using this option, the top edges of the chosen slices are aligned.
- **Align to slice center**: Using this option, you can align to the slice centers you've chosen.
- **Align the bottom edges**: The bottom edges of the chosen slices are aligned using this option.
- **Distribute horizontally**: Using this option, the chosen layers are distributed horizontally.

○ **Show/Hide Auto Slice**: Photoshop makes slices for the remainder of the page whenever we use the Slice tool to make a slice because we already know this. Thus, we can use Photoshop's Show/Hide Auto Slice option to reveal or hide the auto slices it creates.

217

CHAPTER NINE

RETOUCHING TOOLS IN PHOTOSHOP

Image Retouching in Photoshop

What you will learn in this chapter.

- **The numerous terms used when editing photos.**
- **How to utilize all of Photoshop's editing features; Spot, Spot Healing, Healing, Patch, Content-Aware Move, Red Eye, Clone Stamp, Blur, Sharpen, Smudge, Dodge, Burn, Sponge, and more.**
- **The connection between the History Brush Tool and the History Panel.**

This feature in Photoshop is crucial for photography and social media design. Terms like "airbrushing," "post-production," "photo retouching," and "photo editing" are commonly misunderstood when discussing photography. Although these terms all refer to picture alteration, some photographers use them to mean various things. To help you better understand the results you can anticipate from your photography or photo retouching service, we've chosen to go a step further and explain the differences between these expressions.

Photo Retouching

"Photo retouching" refers to removing any flaws from a photograph. Typically, this entails modifying the color and tone, removing dark bags beneath the eyes, and changing the saturation, contrast, and brightness. Additionally, picture retouching occasionally includes airbrushing, which is the act of adding or deleting background elements from the image.

Photo Editing

Photo editing includes cropping, altering exposure, and adjusting color temperature. It should be mentioned that "photo editing" and "photo retouching" are sometimes used interchangeably. Additionally, some photographers claim that editing consists of selecting only the best photos from the gallery after looking through the raw data from the photo shoot.

Photo Enhancing

Generally speaking, photo enhancement refers to improving the overall appearance of the image. Examples include changing the color scheme (to black and white), vignetting, and toning. Enhancement is done after editing to ensure that the colors are uniform throughout the collection and to give each event shot a unique feel.

Post-Production/ Post-Processing

All of the previously covered subjects are referred to as post-production/post-processing. It includes making any changes to the images after they have been captured. Please be aware that the meaning of each sort of post-production service varies depending on the professional. Therefore, to find out exactly what changes will be made to your photos, you would need to chat with your photography or photo-retouching company.

NOTE: All the concepts defined above are mostly used in the photography niche.

Basic Retouching Tools in Photoshop
One of the many tools that Photoshop provides. To add stunning finishing touches to photos, experts use Photoshop's main photo-retouching tools. Retouching photos is made simpler by using these tools, which are located in Photoshop's tools panel. Photoshop's retouching tools include the following: **Blur and Sharpen Tool, The Color Replacement Tool, Red Eye, Patch Tool, Content-Aware Tool, Clone Stamp Tool, Healing Brush Tool, Spot Healing Tool, and Pattern Stamp Tool**.

Working With The Spot Healing Brush
In Photoshop's Tools Menu, the Spot Healing Brush is nestled among other retouching tools, including the Red Eye Tool, Content-Aware Move Tool, Patch Tool, and Healing Brush Tool.

Dust spots and tiny flaws and blemishes can be fixed with the Spot Healing Brush. It is employed to eliminate little items or undesired areas from photos. It is more likely that the Spot Healing Brush will remove the object seamlessly if it is smaller. Additionally, regions with less detail, like the sky or the ocean, benefit more from object removal in photographs.

Follow the instructions below to use this tool.

- ✤ Click the + icon beneath the layer panel to add a new layer after you've opened your image. Why do this? It guarantees that your changes are non-destructible and that your original image is not changed.

- ✤ After creating a blank layer, you can either press J on your keyboard to directly access the spot healing brush or choose it from the tool menu.

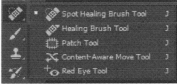

- ✤ After selecting your spot healing brush, adjust its settings in the **Options Bar.** How do I do this?
  - o Be sure that **Sample All layers** are checked.
  - o The mode should be set to **Normal** and the type to **Content-Aware**

  - o The **Brush Angle** does not matter as long as you are using a perfectly round brush.

- ✤ Adjust your brush settings in the brush panel adjacent to **Mode.**

- o You can adjust the brush's size based on what you wish to remove from your photo. Making yourself just large enough to cover the problem without going overboard is the optimal size modification. A 50% hardness and a 25% spacing are ideal for most photographs. To ensure that the brush is correctly rounded, set the roundness parameter to 100%.
- ✦ Then you can start to retouch your image.

Although we have just utilized one type of Spot Healing Brush, you have a few more options to consider.:

- ✦ **Mode**: Among the various modes of operation for the Spot Healing Brush are Normal, Multiply, Screen, Color, and Luminosity. Each of these modes does a few different duties. To put it simply, they tell Photoshop how to make the new pixels look like the old ones. However, it's unlikely that you will ever need to use any of these options to edit your photos.
- ✦ **Type**: This option offers three options: Proximity Match, Content-Aware, and Create Texture.
    - o **Content-Aware**: For spot healing, Content-Aware is usually the best option. Photoshop automatically examines your image in this version of the Spot Healing Brush to identify which pixels should be replaced with the ones you wish to fix.
    - o **Create Texture**: When you use the Create Texture Spot Healing Brush in Photoshop, the pixels around the image you want to replace will form a pattern. This can be very effective for textured patterns that require careful realignment.
    - o **Proximity Match**: Proximity Match examines the pixels just around the region you are fixing to find matching pixels to replace. This version of the Spot Healing Brush works well for spot-healing a small area that precisely matches the surrounding areas.
- ✦ **Spacing**: The spacing option allows you to adjust how smooth the brush looks when you click and drag. At 25%, the majority of photographs will function

perfectly. At zero, the brush will be as smooth as possible. The Spot Healing Brush will have dispersed spots at 1,000% spacing even when you click and drag.

✦ **Angle/Roundness**: The angle and roundness settings let you change the brush's shape. When the brush is perfectly round, it is a perfect circle. On the other hand, reducing the roundness will change the shape of the brush, and adjusting the angle will change the rotation of the oval. This can sometimes help with spot eradication. You won't need to use these choices most of the time.

Working With The Healing Brush

Imperfections, flaws, and uneven skin tones can all be eliminated with the Healing Brush tool. By combining them with the pixels in the surrounding image, it does this. The Healing Brush Tool works similarly to the Clone Stamp tool. In contrast, the Healing Brush Tool also makes sure that the sampled pixels have the same texture, shading, and lighting as the original pixels. Consequently, the replicated pixels blend seamlessly with their new environment.

Follow the instructions below to use this tool.

✦ Make a copy of the original image after opening it, making sure to make all the necessary changes to the copy. Why do this? It guarantees that your changes are non-destructive and that your original image is not changed.

✦ Select the Healing Brush tool 🖌 (J) from the toolbar. Click and hold the Spot Healing Brush tool first if you are unable to locate the Healing Brush tool. Next, select the tool called Healing Brush.

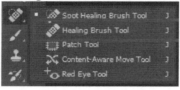

Click the brush sample in the tool options bar to open a pop-up box where you may choose the **Brush Size, Mode, Source, Aligned, Sample**, and **Diffusion** parameters. If needed, adjust its settings in the Options Bar.

✦ .

✦ Ensure that **Sampled** is checked in your **Source option,** Your **Mode** is **Normal** and your **Sample** is in **Current Layer.**

✦ To set the source sampling area, place the pointer over a section of your image and Alt-click (Windows) or Option-click (Mac).
✦ Move your brush over the area you wish to retouch after sampling the selected region as instructed in the previous step. The sampled pixels are added to the existing pixels each time you release the mouse button.

The Healing Brush Option Settings

The Healing Brush tool has several characteristics that you can use to improve your chances of curing specific issues. Once chosen, the healing brush settings are shown in the Options Bar.

✦ **Brush**: Before you can use any tool to paint in Photoshop, you need to choose a brush. Click the brush option to select the tool's brush size, shape, and hardness.

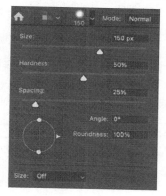

- ○ **Size**: The first thing to look for when choosing a brush for mending is its size. Generally, choose a brush about twice the size of the imperfection at its widest point. Since most scratches are rather small, it will be challenging to keep the sample area from straying over pixels that don't match the area you're attempting to fix if you make the brush too big.
- ○ **Hardness**: To change the hardness of a brush, do the following: The Options bar contains the Brush button.
  Drag the hardness slider to the left to set it to a value less than 100%.
✦ **Mode**: The Healing Brush has several working modes, including Normal, Replace, Multiply, Screen, Darken, Colour, and Luminosity. Each of these modes serves a few distinct purposes. Essentially, they advise Photoshop on how to combine the new and old pixels. You probably won't ever need to edit your images with any of these tools.

✦ **Source**: This determines the source from which you want to pick your sampling region for retouching. There are two options available in the source feature.

    o **Sampled:** allows you to pick any region of your image as a sampling source for healing.

    o **Pattern:** allows you to pick the preset patterns in your Photoshop as a sampling source for healing.

✦ **Aligned**: The Aligned gadget on the Options bar forces the starting point to follow your cursor even after you have finished a stroke. In contrast to leaving it off, which causes the sample point to start at its original location at the beginning of each stroke.

✦ **Use Legacy**: allows you to use the algorithm of the legacy healing brush available in Photoshop CC 2014

✦ **Sample**: allows you to decide the range of layers you want your healing effects to apply either **Current layer, Current & Below, or All layers**

✦ **Diffusion:** When utilizing the healing brush, there is a setting named "diffusion" in the Options Bar. From a drop-down menu, select a number between 1 and 7. How many pixels are spread out around your brush depends on that quantity. The least amount of dispersion occurs when the diffusion is set to 1.

Working With The Patch Tool
Adobe Photoshop has a feature called the Patch Tool that you may use to alter your photographs. Because of their similar purposes, it is a member of the Spot Healing Brush

group. But unlike the Spot Healing Brush, which works by brushing on the image, this tool works by selecting a specific area of the image.

To put it succinctly, the Patch Tool can be used to duplicate and remove items. As previously mentioned, the Patch Tool is used to either fully remove or duplicate items.

To **remove unwanted elements** with the patch tool, follow the procedure below,

- ◆ To retouch an image, open it first. You might as well make a copy of your image and make sure that any changes are made to the copy to protect the original. The copy also acts as a fresh and secure canvas for the experiment.
- ◆ Select the **Patch Tool** from the **Tool Menu** in **The Spot Healing Brush Nest**

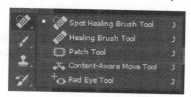

- ◆ Adjust the tool's settings in the **Options bar** if necessary.

- ◆ Ensure that **Source** is checked and **Destination** is left unchecked in the **Options Bar**. **Source** allows you to remove an element completely while **Destinations** clones a selected object.

- ◆ Create a selection around the element you want to remove from the image
- ◆ Drag your selection to the part you want to replace it with. In reality, the area you selected after dragging the initial selection overrides the area you initially selected.

To clone an element with the patch tool, follow the procedure below,

- ◆ Open the picture you wish to edit. To avoid destroying the original image, you might as well make a copy of your image and make sure that all changes are made to it. The copy will act as a fresh and safe canvas for the experiment.
- ◆ Select the **Patch Tool** from the **Tool Menu** in **The Spot Healing Brush Nest**

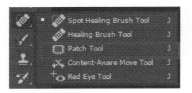

✦ Adjust the tool`s settings in the **Options bar** if necessary.

✦ Ensure that **Destination** is checked while **Source** is left unchecked in the **Options Bar**. **Source** allows you to remove an element completely while **Destinations** clones a selected object.

✦ Create a selection around the image you want to clone.
✦ Drag your selection to any desired region in the image to duplicate it there

The Patch Tool Option Settings

✦ **The Selection Types**: These options determine how your selections interact with each other. They are located at the upper-left of the **Options Bar**.

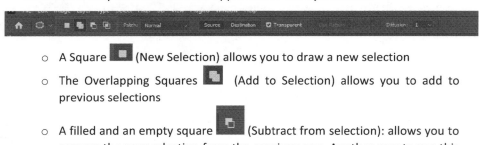

    o A Square ▇ (New Selection) allows you to draw a new selection

    o The Overlapping Squares ▇ (Add to Selection) allows you to add to previous selections

    o A filled and an empty square ▇ (Subtract from selection): allows you to remove the new selection from the previous one. Another way to use this feature is to hold the Alt Key (Windows) or Option Key (macOS) while making a new selection.

    o The Second Overlapping Square ▇ (Overlap Selection): allows you to keep the area shared by the new and previous selections.

✦ **The Content-Aware Patch**: **Normal** and **Content-Aware** are the two options available in the Patch Tool. The Normal mode was employed in the preceding section. The distinction between Normal and Content-Aware is that the patch will produce nearby content when we choose Content-Aware, allowing it to blend in seamlessly with the surrounding content.

On the Content-Aware option bar, there are several options to adjust.

- o **Structure**: Changing the degree to which the patch should replicate current image patterns. The patch adheres strongly to pre-existing image patterns when you set it to maximum (7). The patch only conforms roughly to pre-existing visual patterns when you set it to minimal (1).
- o **Color**: modifying the patch's color blending intensity. Color mixing is disabled if you enter 0. Maximum color blending will be applied if you enter 10.
- o **Sample All Layers**: To generate the move in a different layer utilizing data from all layers, enable this option. In the Layers panel, select the desired layer.

- ⬍ **Source & Destination**: **Source** allows you to remove an element completely while **Destination** clones a selected object.
- ⬍ **Transparency**: When enabled, this option blends the patched part using a transparency factor.
- ⬍ **Pattern**: This choice enables you to patch the area of the image with the preset patterns in your Photoshop.
- ⬍ **Diffusion**: This selection indicates how quickly the patched area catches up to the pixels around it. The better the diffusion, the higher the value. It has a range of 1 to 7 and is set to 5 by default.

Working With Content-Aware Move Tool

You can select an element to move from one picture to another while gently arranging it to look like it belongs there by using the Content-Aware Move tool. Thanks to this application, you can do this without needing to be an expert Photoshop user. Cutting and pasting an image from one picture to another is easy, but changing the appearance so that it doesn't appear "Photoshopped" is a whole other story. In this case, you can use the Content-Aware Move tool.

This tool is located just below your Spot Healing Brush Tool and Patch Tool.

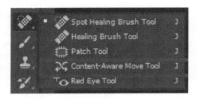

The Content-Aware Tool may be summed up as having two functions: duplicating and moving items. To move an object in Photoshop with ease using the content-aware tool, follow the steps listed below,

❖ Open the picture you wish to alter first. To preserve the original and utilize the copy as a safe and new canvas for experimentation, you might as well create a copy of your image and make sure that all modifications are made to the copy rather than the original.

❖ Select the **Content-Aware Tool** in the **Tool Menu** from the Spot Healing Brush Nest.

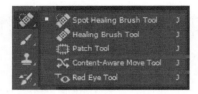

❖ Adjust its settings in the **Options Bar** and let the **Mode** be set on **Move, Transform On Drop** should be checked too

❖ Create a selection around the object you desire to move

❖ Drag the object to the place of your choice and transform it to the size of your choice.

To easily duplicate an object using Photoshop's content-aware tool, follow the steps below.

❖ Open the picture you wish to modify first like you always do. To preserve the original and utilize the copy as a safe and new canvas for experimentation, you might as well create a copy of your image and make sure that all modifications are made to the copy rather than the original.

❖ Select the **Content-Aware Tool** in the **Tool Menu** from the Spot Healing Brush Nest.

- Adjust its settings in the **Options Bar** and let the **Mode** be set on **Extend, Transform On Drop** should be checked too.

- Create a selection around the object you desire to duplicate.
- Drag your selection to the place of your choice and transform it to the size of your choice.

The Content-Aware Tool Option Settings

- **Selection Types**: The selection properties apply to this property as well. There are four selection attributes, and Normal mode is the default setting.

- o **Normal** ▣: This is the selection you make with the content aware tool on a regular basis.
- o More pieces can be added to your patch selection using the **Add to Selection(**▣**)** selection feature than we can with the content-aware tool.
- o **Remove selection (**▣**)**: Using this selection attribute, you can opt to take out some of the already-selected pieces that need to be repaired.
- o **Intersect Selections (**▣**)** Selections that are common to two other selections are taken into account by this attribute, which functions similarly to an intersection.
- **Mode**: This option allows you to explore the two distinct functions of the content-aware tool.
  - o **Move:** This feature allows you to completely move elements in Photoshop
  - o **Extend:** This is a feature in the content-aware tool that allows you to duplicate the elements of an image.

- **Structure**: You can use this tool to manage the final product of your effort. Structure allows you to tell the computer to make the edit's structure as similar to the original texture as feasible.
- **Color**: Color is employed to control the final product of your work, just like structure. You can select the degree to which the color of the content you are moving will match the color of the stuff it is replacing by using color.
- **Sample All layers**: Enable this option to generate the move in a distinct layer using data from all layers, just like it is with other retouching tools. Choose the desired layer in the Layers panel.
- **Transform On Drop**: enables you to adjust the object's size before completing your job.

Working With Red Eye Tool

The red eye tool is used to eliminate the red hue and replace it with a natural black pupil color, as the name suggests. The Red Eye tool is applied to an image of an eye that has red in it.

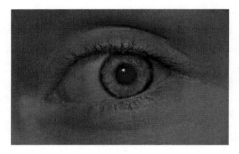

The **Red Eye Tool** is located in the **Tool Menu** in the Spot Healing Brush Nest.

What causes Red Eye?

When taking pictures in low light, the flash is triggered very close to the subject's face. The pupil of the subject reflects the light. Instead of appearing naturally black, the pupils seem brilliant red because to the light bouncing off the blood vessels behind the eyes. It can make your people look like demons, but it's easy to fix once you know what causes it. Red eye is the result of an on-camera flash bouncing off the subject's eyes and appearing in the picture.

How do I use the Red Eye Tool?

- Navigate to the toolbar on the left.
- "Spot Healing Brush Tool" should be selected.
- The "Red Eye Tool" is located at the bottom of the "Spot Healing Brush Tool" menu.

- Make sure Pupil Size and Darken Amount are both set to 50% in the top left-hand corner of the menu. (This is a best practice) Adjust the settings if you want to use a different approach.

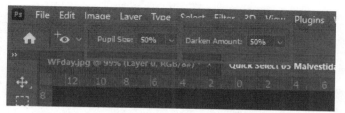

- Finally, Make a selection around the red-eye and then unclick, the red-eye should be gone.

Working With Clone Stamp Tool

When you need to accurately replicate color and detail from one area of an image to another, the Clone Stamp Tool works well. One part of an image can be duplicated onto another part of the same image using Photoshop's Clone Stamp tool. Photographers and designers commonly use the Clone Stamp tool to remove distracting elements from a shot. For example, it can be used to cover up facial defects by copying from another area of the skin or to remove trees from a mountain view by copying parts of the sky over them.

In a nutshell, Photoshop's Clone Stamp is used to duplicate and remove items.

Follow the instructions below to use effectively use the Clone Stamp Tool.

- In Photoshop, open the image you wish to edit. You have two options: either make a fresh copy of your original image and work on it or add a new blank layer.
- Navigate to the **Tool Menu** and select the **Clone Stamp Tool**.

✥ Adjust the tool`s settings at **Option Bar** to suit your desire. If you`re making your modifications to a duplicate copy of the original image, you can set your **sample** at **Current Layer/All layers** but if you`re working on a new blank layer, set your sample at **All layers/Current & Below.**

✥ When the Clone Stamp tool is active, you can set the sample point by Alt-clicking (in Windows) or Option-clicking (in MacOS) a region of detail. The sample point is your source region, which is the area where you are copying the duplicate you wish to make. A preview of the amount of detail you'll need for retouching is shown inside the Clone Stamp pointer. Use the preview to align the sampled detail with other parts of the image.

✥ Lightly brush over the area where you want to add the sampled detail to cover an item. As you work, a crosshair indicates where the detail is copied from.

✥ Examine the results to look for details that are repeated, and then use the clone stamp tool once more to make little changes.

The Clone Stamp Tool Option Settings

✥ **Brush**: You must select a brush in Photoshop before you can paint with any tool. To choose the tool's brush size, shape, and hardness, click the brush option.

- ○ **Size**: The size of the brush is the first consideration while picking one for Cloning
- ○ **Hardness**: To adjust a brush's hardness, take the following actions:
  The Brush button is located on the Options bar.
  Set the hardness slider to a value lower than 100% by dragging it to the left.
- ◆ **Mode**: The Clone Stamp Tool offers a variety of choices, including operating modes. Each of these modes serves a few distinct purposes. Essentially, they advise Photoshop on how to combine the new and old pixels. You probably won't ever need to edit your images with any of these tools.

- **Opacity**: The degree of transparency with which your brush will paint over the selected region is specified by this feature. To change the opacity level, move the Opacity slider.

- **Aligned:** Selecting this option will allow you to continue painting on the freshly cloned image even if you release the mouse button in the middle of it. The clone will begin drawing at the sample point if you release the mouse button and pick up the painting again after it has been deselected.
- **Sample:** determines the layer(s) your cloning will have visible effects on.

- **Flow:** indicates the intensity of the brush you are cloning with. You adjust the slider to make changes to your flow.

Working With Pattern Stamp Brush

The Pattern Stamp tool allows you to fill a selection or layer with a pattern or apply a pattern from the pattern library. Photoshop offers a wide selection of patterns. The Clone Stamp Tool contains the Pattern Stamp Brush. It overlays an image with a chosen pattern.

How do I use The Pattern Stamp Brush?

- From the **Tool Menu**, pick the Pattern Stamp tool. (After selecting the Clone Stamp tool, click the Pattern Stamp tool icon in the Tool Options bar if it isn't visible in the toolbox.)

✦ Choose a pattern from the Tool Options bar's Pattern pop-up menu. You can load a library by selecting its name from the panel menu, or you can select Load Patterns and navigate to the library's folder. You can also design your own pattern.

✦ Then brush your pattern on your image.

The Pattern Stamp Brush Settings

✦ **Brush**: Set the brush tip. After selecting a brush category from the Brush drop-down menu by clicking the arrow next to the brush sample, select a brush thumbnail.

✦ **Impressionist**: Use paint daubers to apply impressionist painting techniques to the pattern.

✦ **Size**: sets the brush's size in pixels. Enter a size in the text box or move the Size slider.

✦ **Opacity**: determines the transparency of the pattern you apply. When the opacity is set to a low value, pixels beneath a pattern stroke can be seen. Enter an opacity value or move the slider.

✦ **Mode**: Indicates how the paint you apply will interact with the picture's existing pixels. Blending modes are discussed there.

✦ **Aligned**: the pattern in a continuous, unified pattern. From one paintbrush stroke to the next, the pattern is in alignment. When you stop and start painting, the pattern will always be centered on the pointer if **Aligned** is deselected.

The Blur Tool, Sharpen Tool, and Smudge Tool
These three tools are nested together in a tool group in Photoshop`s Tool Menu. They are also called the **Focus Tools** These tools are used for retouching in Photoshop.

The uneven areas of an image can be softened or hardened with the "**Blur Tool**." To improve an image's contrast and clarity, utilize the "**Sharpen tool**." To combine the portions of an image, the "**Smudge tool**" is employed. Let's quickly explore each focal tool.

Working With The Blur Tool

The blur tool blurs an image or is typically used to soften an image's sharp pixels. It can also give the image a creative touch, but how it does so will only be determined by how you use the tool.

The contrast between adjacent pixels is lessened when using the blur tool. The blur tool's icon resembles *a droplet of water that is about to fall* ()

The **Options Bar** in the upper side of the workspace contains the settings of the blur tool, like every other tool in Photoshop.

- **Brush**: This tool offers the same brush options as a brush tool or an eraser tool since it applies the effect using the brush tip. Before using any tool in Photoshop, you must first choose a brush. Click the brush option to select the brush's size, shape, and hardness.

- Size: When choosing a brush for cloning, size is the first factor to take into account.
- Hardness: The following steps should be taken to modify a brush's hardness: On the Options bar is where you'll find the Brush button.
Drag the hardness slider to the left to drop the value below 100%.
- **Modes**: The Blur Tool has a number of different choices, including several working modes. Each of these modes carries out a variety of tasks. To put it simply, they advise Photoshop on how to mix in the new and old pixels. You most likely won't ever need to edit images using any of these programs.

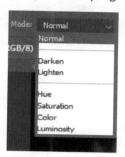

- **Strength**: You can also modify the brush's strength to lessen the blur effect by adjusting the slider or input a specific figure in the slider`s box.

- **Sample All Layers**: Having this effect checked allows your modifications to affect all layers, current, below and above.

How do I use The Blur Tool?

- Open up the image you want to retouch in Photoshop. You can either duplicate your original image and work on your new copy or add a new blank layer to your image. Ensure that **Sample All layers** is checked
- Select the Blur tool from the Tool Menu

✦ Adjust your brush settings in the **Options Bar** if necessary.

✦ Paint your brush over the area you want to modify.

Working With The Sharpen Tool

The second item in the fly-out menu for the blur tool is the sharpen tool. Its icon resembles a pointed triangle (△.).

The sharpen tool improves the pixel contrast and brings more attention to the image. You must be very careful when using this tool because "sharpening" any part of the image will make that part stand out. So be careful not to over-sharpen it.

How do I use The Sharpen Tool?

✦ Like you did for other retouching tools, open up the image you want to retouch in Photoshop. You can either duplicate your original image and work on your new copy or add a new blank layer to your image. Ensure that **Sample All layers** is checked

✦ Select **The Sharpen Tool** from the **Tool Menu** under the **Blur's tool drop-down tool options.**

238

- Adjust the tool`s settings in the **Options Bar** to your desired taste. It is advisable to keep the value of the tool`s strength under 25% to make subtle effects on your work.

- Paint your brush over the area you want to modify.

The Sharpen Tool`s Options Setting

- **Brush**: This tool offers the same brush options as a brush tool or an eraser tool since it applies the effect using the brush tip. Before using any tool in Photoshop, you must first choose a brush. Click the brush option to select the brush's size, shape, and hardness.

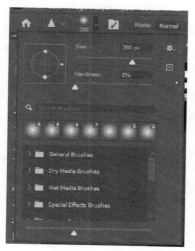

- o Size: When choosing a brush for cloning, size is the first factor to take into account.
- o Hardness: The following steps should be taken to modify a brush's hardness: On the Options bar is where you'll find the Brush button. Drag the hardness slider to the left to drop the value below 100%.
- **Modes**: The Sharpen Tool has a number of different choices, including several working modes. Each of these modes carries out a variety of tasks. To put it simply, they advise Photoshop on how to mix in the new and old pixels. You most likely won't ever need to edit images using any of these programs.

239

- **Strength**: You can also modify the brush's strength to lessen the sharpening effects by adjusting the slider or input a specific figure in the slider's box.

- **Sample All Layers**: Having this effect checked allows your modifications to affect all layers, current, below and above. This option is very useful when you have multiple layers.

- **Protect Detail**: This option applies localized sharpening in a regulated way.

Working With The Smudge Tool

This is the third and last tool in the blur tool's fly-out menu. As it is used to smooth an image, it is fairly similar to the blur tool. In the liquify option, this tool behaves almost like a warping effect.

The Smudge Tool mimics smudging paint with your finger and is designed to be used when painting. similar to how artists work while drawing traditionally. However, the tool can still be utilized to make spot edits.

The pixels are pushed around the canvas like wet paint that is being smudged. Thus, the moniker "smudge tool " was born. If you want to give your image a creative, digitally painted effect, the smudge tool is really helpful.

You choose the layer you want to paint on when using the smudge tool. It blends all the pixels together from when you first started painting.

The Smudge Tool`s Options Setting

- **Brush**: Pick any brush of your choice from the brush presets, and click the brush option to select the brush's size, shape, and hardness.
  - o Size: When choosing a brush for cloning, size is the first factor to take into account. Unlike other retouching tools, The Smudge tool does not consider brush hardness.

- **Mode**: There are numerous options available for the Smudge Tool, including various operating modes. These modes each do different functions. Simply put, they offer Photoshop advice on how to blend in the new and old pixels. Most likely, none of these programs will ever be required for image editing.
- **Strength**: similar to the Sharpen and Blur Tools. The strength setting on the Smudge Tool controls how significantly your strokes will impact the image. More pixels will be moved by your strokes the stronger the strength.

241

- **Sample All Layers**: The sample all layers' option should be selected if your image contains more than one layer so that editing will only be done on the active layer.
- **Finger Painting**: The smudge tool adds a small stroke to the image when this option is checked, which is somewhat helpful if you want to utilize the tool for painting and color blending.

How do I use The Smudge Tool?

- Similar to the blur and sharpen tools, open up the image you want to retouch in Photoshop. You can either duplicate your original image and work on your new copy or add a new blank layer to your image. Ensure that **Sample All layers** is checked
- Select **The Smudge Tool** from the **Tool Menu** under the **Blur`s tool drop-down tool options.**

- Adjust the Tool`s setting in the **Options Bar** if necessary.

- Paint your brush over the area you want to modify.

The Dodge Tool, Burn Tool, and Sponge Tool

Adobe Photoshop's Dodge, Burn, and Sponge tools are great for adjusting the focus point of a shot that didn't work out the way you expected. They are based on conventional darkroom techniques for correcting parts of a photograph that are overexposed or underexposed.

You can access these tools in the Tools Menu on the left side of the Workspace,

The letter **O** serves as the shortcut command to access these utilities. There is a nesting of these three tools.

To put it simply, the Sponge tool saturates or desaturates the color in an area, the Burn tool darkens it, and the Dodge tool lightens it. These parameters also apply to other retouching tools, such as the Healing Brush, Spot Healing Brush, Clone Stamp Tool, Blur Tool, Sharpen Tool, Smudge Tool, etc., but there are certain factors you should know before using them:

- Destructive editing techniques include Dodge, Burn, and Sponge. That suggests that the picture itself is altered directly. For this reason, it's best to avoid working on the background layer. By making multiple layers and working with them, you can eliminate errors if you go too far.
- Due to the fact that these are brushes, you can "paint." You can adjust the brush's size by using the [and [keys, respectively.

Note the following about this Triad tool.

- **Highlights:** consists of the brightest areas and it permits modifications to these areas
- **Shadow:** Unlike the Highlights, it consists of the darkest area of an image and allows changes to be made in these areas.
- **Mid-tones:** are areas that are between the darkest and the brightest areas, more like grey. Like the other features, Mid-tones also permit modifications to their areas.

243

Working With The Dodge Tool

Use Photoshop's Dodge tool to lighten a portion of the image without altering its color or saturation. Additionally, it can be utilized to highlight particular aspects of the picture. Saturation will become noticeable if we use it often, making the dodged areas bright grey. Some artists view the dodge tool as "destructive image manipulation" because changes made with it cannot be undone.

Options Setting of The Dodge Tool

To effectively use the dodge tools in our artwork, we must be aware of a few crucial characteristics.

The properties of the dodge tool are shown below:

❖ **Brush Size**: This parameter allows us to change the brush's size to suit our requirements. You can adjust the brush's size and hardness in a pop-up window that appears when you choose this option.

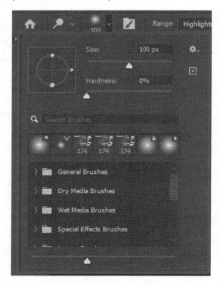

❖ **Brush Setting**: By utilizing this feature, we can provide our brushes with additional choices. As the image below shows, we have a lot of possibilities for our brushes in this brush setting.

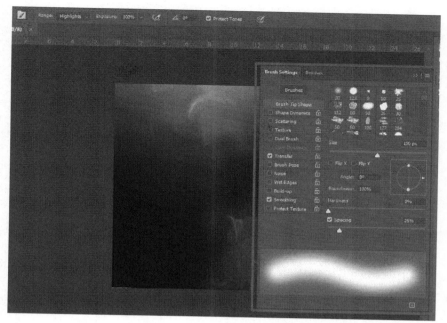

❖ When you select the range option, a drop-down menu will appear with the following three choices:

- **Mid-tones**: This option modifies the grayscale's middle tonal range. It is the range's default choice.
- **Shadows**: This setting modifies the image's shadows.
- **Highlights**: This choice modifies the image's bright regions.

❖ **Exposure**: Similar to how exposed a photograph would be, this parameter controls how powerful the tool's impact will be. Although the slider's default value is 50, depending on the circumstance, it can range from 0 to 100.

- **Airbrush**: This option is utilized for airbrushes. Choose this option if you wish to utilize an air brush. It will refine your brush.

- **Protect tone**: This option retains the image's tonal quality during lightning, which will stop the colors from shifting in hue.

How Do I use The Dodge Tool?

- Open the image you want to modify in Photoshop
- Choose the dodge tool from the **Tool Bar** but before using it, make a copy of your layer because the dodge tool's effects are irreversible.
- Adjust the tool`s settings in the **Options Bar** to your satisfaction.
- Paint your brush over the region of the image you desire to modify.

Working With The Burn Tool
The Burn tool achieves nearly the same but opposite outcomes as the Dodge tool and is typically used in conjunction with it. This is an explanation of Burn, its benefits, and its connection to Dodge.

In essence, burn darkens the pixels you paint. The Burn tool will ultimately turn a color entirely black, as if you had burned it if you use it for a long enough amount of time. Dark shadows can be produced with a burn. The Dodge and Sponge Tools and the Burn Tool are nestled together in the Tool Bar.

,

The settings for the burn tool are displayed in the **Options Bar.**

The Options Of The Burn Tool

We need to be aware of a few key qualities in order to apply the burn tools on our artwork properly.

⬍ **Brush Size**: We can adjust the brush size to meet our needs by using this option. Selecting this option opens a pop-up box where you may adjust the brush's size and hardness.

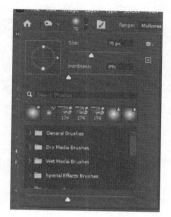

⬍ **Brush Setting**: By using this attribute, we can provide our brushes with additional options. As the image below shows, we have a lot of options for our brushes in these brush settings.

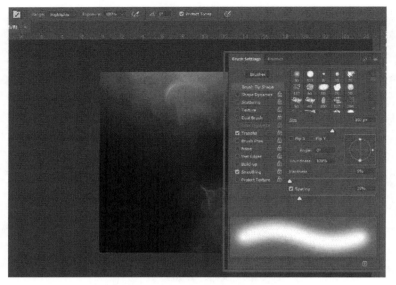

✦ **Range**: The following three options will be available in a drop-down menu when you choose the range option:

   o **Mid-tones**: This setting alters the middle tonal range of the grayscale image. It is the default option for the range.
   o **Shadows**: This option changes the shadows in the image.
   o **Highlights**: This option changes the bright areas of the image.

✦ **Exposure**: We can adjust the brush size to meet our needs by using this option. Selecting this option opens a pop-up box where you may adjust the brush's size and hardness

✦ **Airbrush**: This choice is used with airbrushes. If an air brush is what you want to use, pick this option. It will make your brush better.

✦ **Protect tone**: This choice prevents color gradation by maintaining the image's tonal quality during lightning.

How do I use The Burn Tool?

✦ In Photoshop, open the picture you want to work on.
✦ From the Tool Bar, choose the sponge tool. Because the effects of the burn tool are irreversible, make a copy of your layer before using it.
✦ Using the Options Bar, change the tool's parameters as needed. Paint the desired portion of the image with your brush.

Working With The Sponge Tool

Color saturation is impacted by Photoshop's sponge tool. A hue may become more or less saturated as a result. This implies that we can use the sponge tool to either increase or decrease the intensity of the colors of certain pixels. The dodge and burn tool and the sponge tool are nested together.

The Options Bar on the top side of the Photoshop workspace shows the sponge tool's options.

To understand how the sponge tool works, you must first understand the two modes that are available in the properties bar beneath the menu bar :

249

You can see the two modes in the aforementioned image:

- **Saturate Mode**: This increases the color intensity of the pixels.
- **De-saturate Mode**: This lowers the color intensity of the pixels.

Option Settings of The Sponge Tool

Let's now examine how the sponge tool functions.

- **Brush Preset Picker**: This feature enables us to select the brush type we desire.

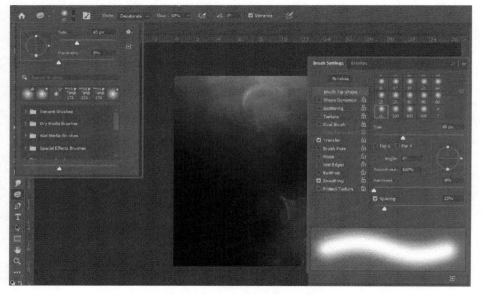

- **Mode**: The most significant characteristic of the sponge tool is its mode. The Sponge tool has two modes: Desaturate and Saturate, as we've already covered.
  - o Desaturate: In this mode, the image's colors are less intense. (That is, it lessens the color's intensity when applied.)
  - o Saturate: This mode enhances the image's color.

✤ **Flow**: This option determines the amount of saturation or desaturation that will take place when we use the sponge tool. Its range of values is 0 to 100%.

✤ **Vibrance**: The vibrancy of the image is preserved while using the sponge tool when this option is used. It is crucial to keep the sponge tool under observation when utilizing it.

✤ **Pen Pressure Size**: Only users of a graphics tablet are eligible for this feature, which allows for pressure-based brush size adjustment.

How do I use the Sponge Tool?

✤ Open the image you desire to edit in Photoshop
✤ From the Tool Bar, choose the sponge tool. Make a copy of your layer before utilizing the sponge tool because its effects are permanent.
✤ Adjust the tool`s settings in the **Options Bar** for the modifications you desire to make.
✤ Paint the portion of the image you want to edit using your brush.

Other Retouching Tools – Working With The Brush Tools

Although it is a tool in and of itself, Photoshop's brush tool also acts as a nest for other related tools. The Brush tool contains the Mixer Brush Tool, the Pen Tool, the Colour Replacement Tool, and itself.

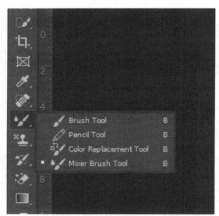

Other brush tools are The History Brush Tool and the Art History Brush Tool, but these tools are nested outside the brush tool.

In this section, we will be studying each of these tools individually and their specific importance to designing and Photography.

The Brush Tool

Like a real paintbrush, you may use the Brush tool to paint on any layer. Furthermore, you will have access to multiple settings that will enable you to customize it for a range of situations. You'll find that many other tools, such as the Eraser and the Spot Healing Brush, use a set of very similar characteristics once you learn how to use the Brush tool. Painting in your document is made easy with the Brush tool. Locate and choose the Brush tool from the Tools menu, then just click and drag in the document window to paint. You can always use the **B** key on your keyboard to select the Brush tool.

How to use The Brush Tool

- Open a file or picture in Photoshop.
- From the toolbar, pick the Brush tool. As shown in the above image, it may be found on the application's left side.

- The Foreground Color, which is the color at the top of the **Color Picker Tool**, should be clicked before selecting a new brush color from the dialog box.

- Adjust your brush settings in the **Options Bar** to your desired taste.

- Simply hold down the left mouse button while dragging the mouse over the image or document after choosing the tool. You only need to press a button for it to begin painting in order to use it.

Options of Brush Tool

We must be aware of a few options the brush tool offers in order to use it effectively in our artwork.

- **Brush Size**: This feature of the brush tool allows us to change the brush's size to meet our needs. To change the brush size, either right-click the image or document or use the brush picker drop-down option. After that, you have the option of changing the brush's size using the supplied slider or entering the necessary value in the input box.

  There is a shortcut for changing the brush size, which is to utilize the keyboard's pair of brackets for increasing (]) and decreasing (]). ([ ).
- **Brush Hardness**: The intensity of the brush we use to paint is referred to as brush hardness; a softer brush would have smoother edges, whilst a harder brush would have sharper edges. **Hardness**, the second slider, is located in the same drop-down menu as the first one. From there, we may modify our brush's bristles.

- **Brush List**: We may also see a list of several brush types in the same drop-down. Photoshop comes with a variety of brushes that we can choose from based on our needs.

- **Brush Settings**: The symbol for brush settings appears after the brush-picker dropdown icon. Here, we may set up some extra options for our brushes and experiment with them to produce fantastic results for our artwork.

We have a wide variety of options to play with while building up brushes. Here, for instance, we can modify the brush's noise or texture. Additionally, we have a softness slider right here, from which we can only modify the brush's softness.

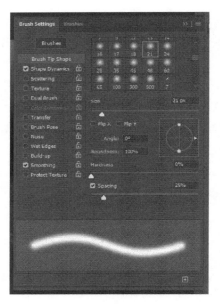

✦ **Blend Modes**: Photoshop's blend mode is a major problem, but we may also reach it here in the brush tool selection. Thus, modifying the mixing of two distinct brush strokes is the primary purpose of blend mode. Depending on our needs, we can select from a few different mixing options in the blend mode drop-down menu.

✦ **Brush Opacity**: We may control the visibility of our brushstrokes by using opacity. The opacity slider's value can be changed from 0% to 100%. Low visibility is indicated by poor opacity, while good visibility is indicated by high opacity.

- **Brush Flow**: Another important feature of brushes is their flow. It just describes the amount of color that can flow when painting. We can prevent it by using a low flow value, which will result in a better outcome and a lower intensity of color flow. More color will flow through our brush if it is high, which could lead to messiness. Furthermore, the flow has values between 0% and 100%, or we can use a slider.

The Pen Tool

The pencil tool is a component of brush tools. The pencil tool is just the tip of a thin, fine brush and shares all the same properties as a brush, except for flow.

The brush tool and the pencil tool are nested together. Shift +B is the shortcut to bring up the pencil tool. The pencil tool is used to create freehand drawings; it is not a retouching tool.

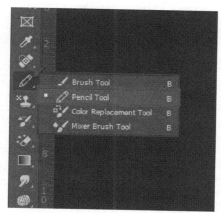

Options Of The Pencil Tool

- **Pencil Size**: The tool's default tip size of one pixel is shown when you select the Brush Preset Picker option from the Options Bar. The user can change the size of the Pencil Brush's tip by clicking the thumbnail or the arrow in the Brush Box

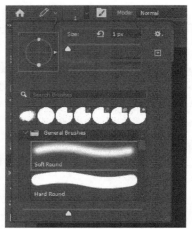

There is a shortcut for changing the brush size, which is to utilize the keyboard's pair of brackets for increasing (]) and decreasing ([). ([ ).

✦ **Brush Hardness**: Brush hardness refers to the intensity of the pencil tip we use to paint; a harder brush would have sharp edges, whilst a softer brush would have smooth edges. The second slider, titled **Hardness**, can be found in the same drop-down as above. From there, we may adjust the bristles of our brush.

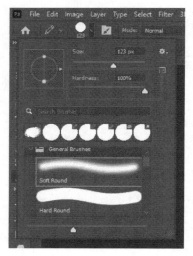

✦ **Brush List**: A drop-down menu may also contain a list of various brush types that we may use for our pencil tool. Depending on our demands, we can choose from a number of brushes that Photoshop includes.

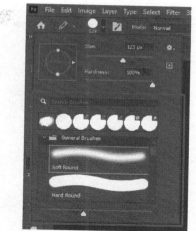

♦ **Brush Settings**: The symbol for brush settings appears after the brush-picker dropdown icon. Here, we may set up some extra options for our brushes and experiment with them to produce fantastic results for our artwork.

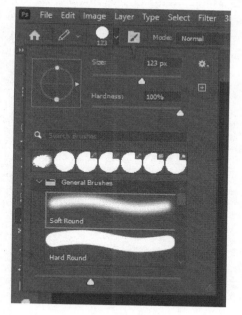

As we build up brushes, we have a lot of alternatives to experiment with. For example, we can change the texture or noise of the brush here. Furthermore, we have a softness slider here that allows us to change merely the brush's softness.

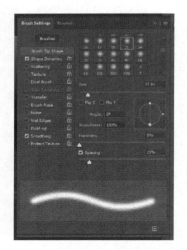

✦ **Blend Modes**: The user can choose between Blend and Other than Normal Mode from the Mode Menu. Numerous techniques for combining colors are made possible by the mix mode. In the Layers Panel, the user must adjust the opacity and mode of the brush pencil on the drawing layer. This gives the user total control over the layer and allows them to make changes at any time

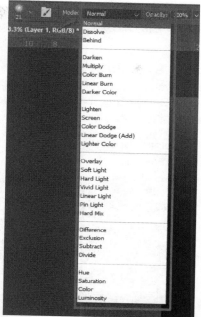

✦ **Brush Opacity**: Opacity enables us to manage how visible our brushstrokes are. We can adjust the value of the opacity slider from 0% to 100%. Poor opacity indicates low visibility, whereas high opacity indicates high visibility.

✦ **Smoothing**: is an option that influences the brush strokes. If checked, reduces the shakiness of brush strokes.

✦ **Auto Erase**: draws background color over the foreground color when activated.

How to use The Pencil Tool

✦ Create a new document if you are not using it on an image or create a new layer for drawing if you are using it on an artwork in Photoshop.
✦ Select your Pencil tool from the brush tool nest in the Tool Bar

261

- ✦ Adjust the tool's settings in the Options Bar to meet your specifications.
- ✦ You can now make freehand drawings with your pencil tool.

Color Replacement Tool

The user can choose between Blend and Other than Normal Mode from the Mode Menu. Numerous techniques for combining colors are made possible by the mix mode. In the Layers Panel, the user must adjust the opacity and mode of the brush pencil on the drawing layer. This gives the user total control over the layer and allows them to make changes at any time. The color substitution tool's icon or symbol is 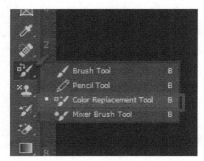. The Color Replacement Tool is nested in the brush tool with other tools in the Tool Bar.

Disadvantages of a color replacement tool:

It can quickly change the image's color, however, it has several accuracy and brightness problems. The more accurate technique used by specialists is adjustments > hue/saturation. This makes the changes more accurate and true to color. Despite this, the color substitution tool is still strongly recommended for beginners and students studying Photoshop.

Options of the Color Replacement Tool

The color replacement tool icon now displays an option bar with a wide range of possibilities when clicked.

.

- ✦ **Brush Size**: The first one (i.e., the one on the far left) is the brush size, where we may adjust the brush's size, hardness, and angle. If you select it, the following dialog box will appear:

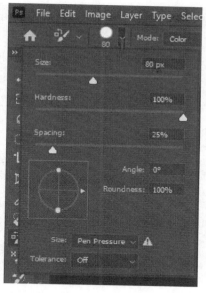

- ○ **Size**: To alter the brush's size.
- ○ **Hardness**: To modify the brush's hardness.
- ○ **Spacing**: Increased spacing will result in discontinuous brushstrokes that are spaced apart from one another. (Use only when necessary)
- ○ **Angle**: The brush's angle is modifiable.
- ○ **Pen Pressure**: Since a graphics tablet is required to view it, it is not utilized here.
- ◆ **Mode**: This is one of the color replacement tool's most crucial characteristics. Tools for replacing colors come in four different mode types.
  - ○ **Color**(Default): This is the color substitution tool's default mode. In this mode, the user's chosen color is simply substituted for the color of the selected area of the image, just like in the article's example.
  - ○ **Hue**: In this option, the hue of the image's selected area is altered.
  - ○ **Saturation**: By changing the color saturation with a less saturated color, this mode can be used to make an image appear dull or bright. By replacing the color saturation with a highly saturated color, this mode can make an image appear bright.
  - ○ **Luminosity**: This setting aids in altering an image's luminosity, or light, to make it bright or dull. Since it frequently degrades the quality of the image, this mode is not recommended for use.

263

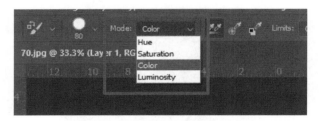

✦ **Sampling**: The names and descriptions of the three sampling choices are as follows (clockwise from the left):

- o **Continuous Sampling**: With this sampling option, the color replacement tool continuously samples the color as we paint.

- o **Once**: In this kind of sampling option, the color replacement tool takes a single sample of the color and then replaces it with the user-selected color wherever it appears.

- o **Background**: In this sort of sampling option, the tool substitutes the sampled color for the background color.

✦ **Limits**: Limits are the next color substitution choice. This option instructs the color replacement as to how far it may modify the color. Photoshop has three limits mode:

- ○ **Contiguous**: When using this limit option, the tool only changes the color of the pixels in the sampled area that are directly under the cursor. It does not alter the color of the nearby pixels that have the same hue.
- ○ **Dis-contiguous**: With this limit type, the tool modifies the color of the immediate surroundings with a matching sampled color up to the spread of the cursor boundary.
- ○ **Find edges**: In this option, the tool discovers the picture's edges automatically and slows down as we get closer to them, limiting the color change to the edges.

✦ **Anti-alias**: Anti-aliasing is the color replacement tool's final feature. Despite the fact that it's not a new tool. It is present in a wide variety of other tools, including erasers and selection tools. Photoshop's anti-alias feature makes it possible to soften the borders of the converted area. Anti-aliasing is turned on by default. Additionally, keeping anti-alias on is advised to provide a perfect color transition at the image's edges.

How do I use The Color Replacement Tool?

✦ Open up your image in Photoshop
✦ Create a selection around the region you want to edit with any selection tool
✦ Select the Color Replacement tool from the Menu Bar

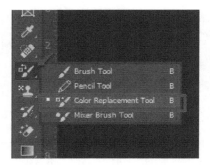

✦ Adjust the tool`s settings in the Options Bar to you desired taste.

✦ Pick the Color you want to replace with from the Color Picker or you pick from the surrounding colors with the eyedropper tool

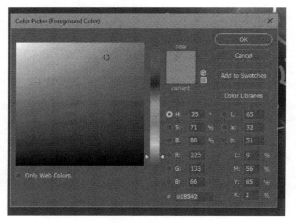

✦ Apply your brush to replace the colors you desire.

Mixer Brush Tool

Because digital painters and illustrators use the Mixer Brush tool so frequently, it is also called "Painter's Paradise." Photo editors also use the mixer brush tool in a variety of ways, and one of its most important uses is skin retouching. Using the mixer brush tool is like painting on a real canvas because it mimics using a real paintbrush. The background color and the brush color are blended, or, to put it another way, you can mix colors as you paint by selecting a sample color from the image you are working on and adjusting the rate at which the brush absorbs color from the image and the rate at which the paint dries. You may find this tool in the brush tool area.

266

In Photoshop, the "Tools" panel is where you can find the Mixer Brush tool. It appears as a paintbrush with a double circle icon ✔ next to it as the fourth tool from the top in the brush tool nest.

The tool`s settings are displayed on the Options bar on the upper side of Photoshop`s workspace.

Options of The Mixer Brush Tool

These options help it become a very powerful tool. When we select the mixer brush tool, the choice bar shows, as seen below:

- **Brush Size**: Every brush tool has an identical option. With this option, we may alter the brush's size, angle, and sharpness.

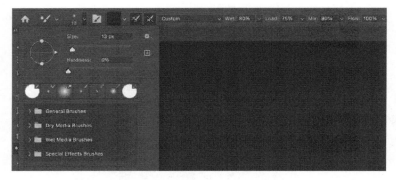

✦ **Current Brush Load**: This option shows the currently loaded color of the brush. It now has interesting properties, and clicking on it opens up other options, as mentioned below.

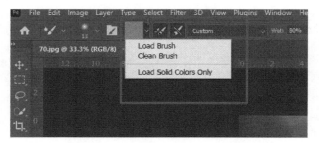

- ○ **Load Brush**: Reload the brush with color using the load option.
- ○ **Clean Brush**: This choice cleans the brush.
- ○ **Load Solid Color Only**: When the box labeled "Load Solid Color Only" is selected, the brush will only load solid colors.
  The question of whether the brush can select anything other than the solid color may now be raised. True is the response.

✦ **Load the brush after each stroke**: The brush will automatically reload with the same color after each stroke if this option is left checked.

✦ **Clean the brush after each stroke**: The brush will automatically clean itself after each stroke if this option is left checked.

- **Presets**: These options have a number of pre-defined functions that were constructed by setting various Wet, load, and mix values. It is set to custom by default, allowing us to design our own preset. If you choose the option, something similar will appear:

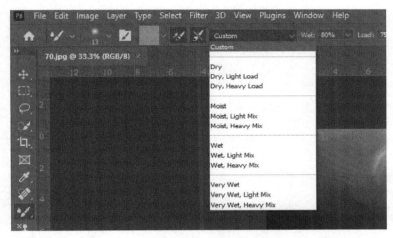

- **Wet**: The value of this option is between 0% and 100%. The mix option is also active when the wet value is set to greater than zero. The amount of paint that the brush removes from the canvas is indicated by this setting. When the mixture is less moist and more blended, there is less color mixing.

- **Load**: Additionally, the value of this option ranges from 0% to 100%. This option shows how much paint is on our brush right now. The amount of paint on the brush increases with the value. As we paint with it, the color load decreases, much like with a real brush. If we set the Wet and Mix parameters to 0 and the load to 100%, we obtain a brush that resembles a normal paintbrush.

269

✤ **Mix**: Additionally, the value of this option ranges from 0% to 100%. This option indicates the amount of colour that mixes with the canvas colours when we paint with a brush. This option is only enabled when wet has a value larger than 0 because we already know that if wet is set to 0, the brush won't pick up any colour.

✤ **Flow**: The value of this option likewise ranges from 0% to 100%. This parameter controls the speed at which the color spreads over each stroke. When the stroke has a larger flow rate, more color is created. The default setting for the flow is 100%.

✤ **Smoothing**: The amount by which it will lessen the shakiness in the brush stroke depends on the value that is selected.

✤ **Sample All layers**: The brush will act as if it is painting on a single layer of canvas even if there may be multiple layers if this option is checked. The tool merges all the layers into one and paints with it even though it has several layers. The option to sample all layers is always selected by default.

270

How do I use the Mixer Brush Tool?

As was already mentioned, the background color and brush color are combined using the mixer brush tool. Let's now examine this in greater detail.

- Open a new document of Adobe Photoshop
- Use the regular brush tool to paint a part of the document with any color of your choice.

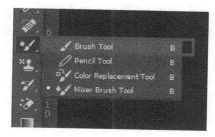

- Select the Mixer Brush from the Tool Menu

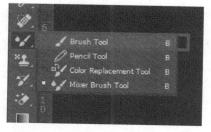

- Adjust the brush`s settings in the Options bar if necessary.

- Select a new color from the Color picker now (different from the color that you have previously chosen).

271

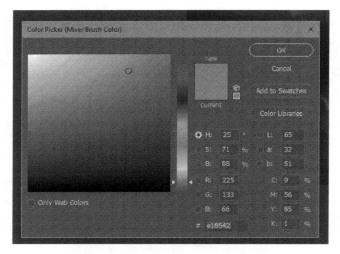

✦ Simply paint over the previous painting and you will get the result of using the mixer brush tool.

History Brush Tool
You can use the History Brush tool to paint over portions of an image to return them to a previous history state. You must comprehend how the History panel influences the history brush's capabilities to use it efficiently.

The History Panel in Photoshop
A history or log of every action performed on the current Photoshop file since its creation is shown in a panel in Photoshop known as the History Panel. As shown below, the history panel can be accessed from the right side of the documents or through the **Window menu** > History.

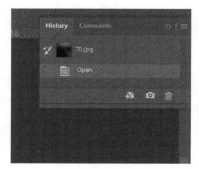

As seen in the image above, the history panel shows all of the changes and work that have been made to the current Photoshop file. In the image above, the snapshot button is a small icon that is red-highlighted. By selecting this option, we can capture a screenshot of a Photoshop document at a particular moment throughout the entire session. Instead of having to start from scratch if something goes wrong or is damaged, the user can choose a point from which to restart work.

Using The History Brush Tool

We now understand the purpose of the history panel. The use of the History brush tool will now be discussed. If you do not have a history of works on your image, the history brush tool will not operate.

- Launch the image's Photoshop file.
- Choose the History brush tool from the Tool Menu on the left side of Photoshop's workspace if you want to restore a portion of your image to its original state after making changes to it.

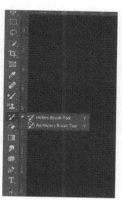

⬍ When you want to go back in history to the initial default image, you will see that the cursor has been changed to a brush. Simply brush over the desired areas.

Properties of The History Brush Tool

The properties/settings of the history brush tool are displayed on the Options bar like every other tool in Photoshop.

We can see a lot of properties here. Let's now examine each of these characteristics individually.

Note: In Adobe Photoshop, the History Brush tool's settings are identical to those of the Normal Brush tool.

⬥ **Mode**: This sets the brush's mode; we can choose from a variety of modes by selecting the mode option, as illustrated below:

Normal is the mode's default setting. You can choose modes based on your needs.

⬥ **Opacity**: The opacity controls how opaque the brush is. Its value falls between 0 and 100%. The brush's opacity is set to 100% by default.

♦ **Flow**: The brush effect's flow is determined by the flow (color in the case of the normal brush).

♦ **Pressure Control Size**: This choice is only applicable if you're using a graphics tablet with adjustable pressure. if you have this option turned on and you're using a graphics tablet. The size of your brush will then adjust based on how hard you press on the tablet.

The Art History Brush Tool

The Art History Brush tool in Adobe Photoshop is an intriguing substitute for the default History Brush tool. Both tools paint over an image by reusing data from a previous state. To give your artwork a brush-stroke appearance, the Art History Brush tool provides several options on the Options bar. The History brush tool in the Tool Menu is nestled inside the Art History brush.

Option Settings of the Art History Brush Tool

This feature of the art history brush tool is displayed on the Options bar like every other tool in Photoshop.

✦ The brush settings in this tool are similar to that of a regular brush.

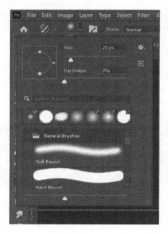

✦ **Mode**: This determines the brush's mode; by selecting the mode option, as seen below, we can select from several options.

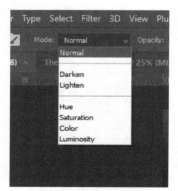

✦ **Style**: Different-shaped brush stroke designs, such as Tight short, Loose Medium, Dab, or Loose Curl, etc. are available in the Style menu.

276

✦ **Area**: Independent of the brush size you choose, this selection determines the area that the paint stroke covers. Greater area coverage is achieved with larger brush sizes.

✦ **Tolerance**: You can adjust how much of a change is made to your photo with this option. Using a smaller tolerance value allows you to apply strokes wherever in the image, independent of the color values. A high tolerance value makes the difference between your image and the original much less noticeable by limiting Art History strokes to regions that deviate greatly from the source state or image.

✦ **Opacity**: determines the transparency of the brush you are drawing with.

277

Working with The Eraser Tool

Because Photoshop has so many tools, it could be challenging to determine which one to use for a certain task or effect. After seeing the tiny rubber in your toolbar, you have undoubtedly wondered a little bit about it. The Eraser Tool in Photoshop has certain benefits, but it also has some disadvantages.

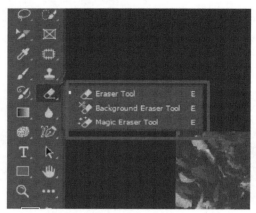

The Eraser, **Background Eraser**, and **Magic Eraser** are the three options available when using the Eraser tool. Using the Pencil has an auto-erase feature as well.

However, it is important to keep in mind that the Eraser tool is destructive. This suggests that your work is irrevocable whenever you utilize the Eraser tool. To restore it, you must continually tell Photoshop to "Undo." If you discover your error after you've saved, you'll most likely need to start over. Think about the Eraser tool as a conventional eraser. If you wipe something in the real world, it's gone.

You may be asking how to remove things from your image that you don't want if you don't want to work destructively. Just apply a layer mask to a layer and use the Brush tool to mask it to modify it.

However, it is important to keep in mind that the Eraser tool is destructive. This suggests that your work is irrevocable whenever you utilize the Eraser tool. To restore it, you must continually tell Photoshop to "Undo." If you discover your error after you've saved, you'll most likely need to start over. Think about the Eraser tool as a conventional eraser. If you wipe something in the real world, it's gone.

You may be asking how to remove things from your image that you don't want if you don't want to work destructively. Just apply a layer mask to a layer and use the Brush tool to mask it to modify it,

✦ Open the image you want to modify in Photoshop. By default, your opened image appears locked in the background layer.

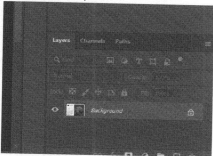

✦ It will look like you are painting with ground color while you are erasing if you want to use your eraser tool on a locked image without first unlocking the background layer. Unlock your layer to make it concealed so that the chequerboard pattern underneath can be seen.

✦ if you are working on a smart object image. It must be rasterized before the rubber tool can be used.

✦ Once the aforementioned has been arranged, select the brush, pencil, or block modes based on the effect you desire. While brushes have rounded, soft edges and pencils have more drawn-line appearances, blocks are square and have harsh edges.

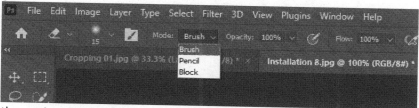

✦ In the settings **Option bar**, you must configure the **opacity** and **flow** when using the brush or pencil modes. Opacity describes the degree of erasure you desire for the pixels. For instance, opacity at 100% will fully remove images while opacity at lower levels will only partially do so.

279

Erase to History: This option in the option bar erases area options designated states.

✦ Drag the cursor across the areas you want to remove while keeping it down.

The Eraser tool is just a brush. You can change the size, hardness, and spacing, just like you would with any brush. You can also choose to change the mode from Brush to Block or Pencil. Instead of painting on the unwanted pixels in your image, the Eraser eliminates them. The only way to recover those permanently erased pixels is to choose "Undo.

Follow the procedures below, to use the **background eraser tool** effectively,

✦ Select the layer containing the regions you want to remove from the Layers panel.
✦ When the option appears, keep holding down the Eraser tool and select Background Eraser.

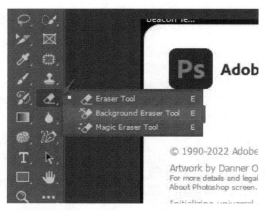

✦ Select a brush and alter the size, hardness, angle, roundness, and spacing settings.
✦ Choose the **Limits mode**
   ○ **Discontiguous**: Wherever the sampled color appears beneath the brush, discontiguous removes it.
   ○ **Contiguous** eliminates sampling color in related areas.
   ○ With **Find Edges**, related regions that have the sample color are removed while edges' shapes are preserved.

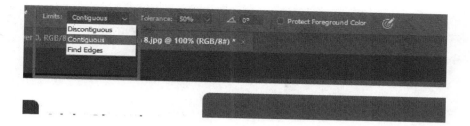

- **Tolerance level** can be chosen by dragging the slider. Compared to low tolerance, which looks for colors that are extremely similar to the sample color, high tolerance will delete a larger spectrum of hues.

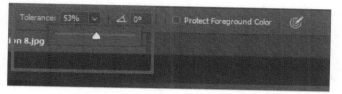

- To prevent accidentally removing the foreground colors, choose **Protect Foreground Color.**

- Decide on a sampling strategy
  - If you choose Continuous, the eraser tool will continuously sample colors while you are dragging it
  - Only the color you first click on will be erased.
  - Any spots that contain the background color will be removed by Background Swatch.

The Eraser tool and the Background Eraser tool are not interchangeable. The tool and cursor will transform into a circle with a + sign in the center when you click. By default, the Background Eraser tool samples the color just below the + in the circle's center. Photoshop will therefore remove all of that color from the bigger circle.

The **Background Eraser options** are shown below,

- ⬍ The first choice is to alter the "brush's" size.
- ⬍ You can select whether you want the Background Eraser to operate **continuously**, **once**, or through a **swatch** using the second option, which begins with two eyedroppers and a gradient below.
    - o The word "**continuous**" was used in the dog photo. When attempting to remove a backdrop with multiple colors, the continuous option performs well.
    - o When you click **once**, the color will be erased as instructed. The color that Photoshop knows to save and remove when you start rotating the circle around the image is where the + is when you click.
    - o With the Tools palette's **Background swatch** option, you can specify a background color that the Background Eraser will only remove.
- ⬍ The Limits section is the next one, and it offers the **Contiguous**, Discontiguous, and **Find Edges options**
    - o **Contiguous**: Only pixels near the pixel beneath the + will be erased by contiguous. The Contiguous option can be annoying if you need to remove something that has obstacles, like hair or branches.
    - o Even if they are not in the same region as the +, the **Discontiguous** option will remove all pixels that match the color you are erasing.
    - o **Find Edges** performs exactly what its name implies; it erases up to the edges that it discovers.
- ⬍ **Tolerance** is the next section in the Background Eraser settings. In other words, the higher the tolerance setting, the more variations of the sampled color Photoshop will be deleted. If the color of your background is similar to the object you don't want to remove, you'll need a low tolerance. In any case, it's a good idea to start low and work your way up.
- ⬍ When you choose **Protect Foreground Color** from the Tools palette, Photoshop will shield the foreground color from erasure. The Protect Foreground Color

checkbox should be selected if the object you're seeking to protect is almost identical to the backdrop but somewhat dissimilar in color.

Follow the procedures below, to use the **Magic Eraser tool**.

✦ The Magic Eraser tool is selected from the toolbar

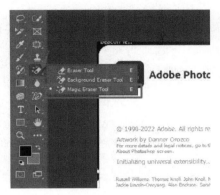

✦ Select a tolerance number. Low tolerance just erases colors that are comparable to the one you've chosen, whereas high tolerance erases a wide range of colors.

✦ If you want sharp edges, choose Anti-Aliased.

✦ Depending on whether you want to delete only adjacent pixels or all similar pixels, choose or deselect **Contiguous**.

✦ To view a sample of the color that was wiped from visible layers, select Sample All Layers.

✦ Select and modify Opacity.

✦ To delete a portion of the layer, click the desired area.

Similar to the Magic Wand tool, the Magic Eraser tool selects a bigger region depending on pixel contrast. The Magic Eraser works precisely like the Magic Wand tool, where you use it and then hit erase. It seems easy to use the Magic Eraser. When you click where you want to erase anything in Photoshop, all of the pixels in that area that are that color will be instantly deleted.

CHAPTER TEN

FILTERS IN PHOTOSHOP

Introduction to Photoshop Filters

One of Adobe's most crucial tools is the Photoshop filter, which can change an image's mood and style while adding distinctive effects. To lessen distortions and improve image quality, professional photographers, graphic designers, and photo editors are the main users. It is also used for projects by hobbyists and amateurs. The majority of third-party filters that are available on the internet are plug-ins. To meet your demands, you can utilize the variety of filters offered by the software itself.

Photoshop filters allow you to swiftly alter the contents of layers. Basic effects like image sharpening and stylization (such as enhancing the edges with a glow or producing a craquelure appearance) are included. Applying a high-pass filter or changing the image's pixel layout are two examples of more complex effects made possible by specific filters.

Filters have an impact on the active layer or the active selection's layer mask. The filter is applied to the layer mask or the layer as a whole if there is no selection.

You can utilize filters without doing any damage by adding Smart Filters to Smart Objects. The original image data stored in the Smart Object can be used at any moment to update the Smart Filters. Smart Filters are saved as layer effects in the Layers panel. for additional details on nondestructive editing and smart filter effects.

To use a filter, choose the appropriate submenu command from the Filter menu. These suggestions can assist you in selecting filters:

- A subset of the visible, active layer is subjected to filters.
- With the Filter Gallery, the majority of filters can be applied cumulatively to images that have 8 bits per channel. You can use each filter separately.

- Filters cannot be applied to images in bitmap mode or indexed color.
- Some filters work only with RGB images.
- Any filter can be used to process 8-bit images.
- The following filters can be applied to 16-bit images: Box Blur, Gaussian Blur, Lens Blur, Motion Blur, Radial Blur, Surface Blur, Shape Blur, Lens Correction, Liquify, Vanishing Point, Average Blur, Blur, Blur More, Clouds, Difference Clouds, Lens Flare, Add Noise, Despeckle, Dust & Scratches, Median, Reduce Noise, Sharpen, Sharpen Edges, Sharpen More,
- The following filters can be applied on 32-bit images: Add NTSC Colors, Emboss, High Pass, Maximum, Minimum, Offset, Clouds, Lens Flare, Smart Sharpen, Unsharp Mask, De-Interlace, and Noise.
- Certain filters are processed entirely in RAM. If not enough RAM is available to process a filter effect, a notification could show up.

The Menu where all filters are nested in the **Filter Menu** in the **Menu bar.**

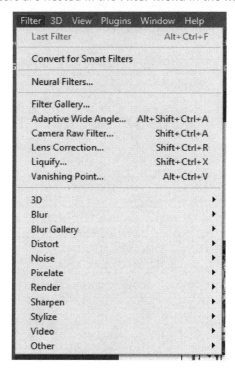

Knowing How to use Filters in Photoshop

There are different filters in the Filter Menu, some of which are grouped together. Some aren't. In Photoshop, there are two kinds of filters: **Extended filters** and **Filter Gallery**. Other filters are available separately.

Extended Filters

No other category applies to the extra filters referred to as extended filters. These are more modern filters with advanced filter effect groups, computations, and pixel analysis.

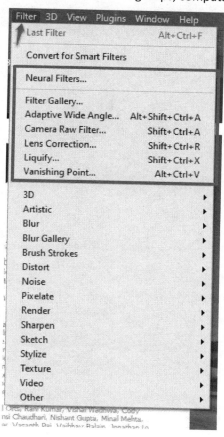

Neural filters, filter galleries, adaptive wide angle, camera raw filters, lens correction, liquefaction, and disappearing point are examples of extended filters.

Using The Neural Filters

Neural filters are a quick and enjoyable approach to enhance your image editing skills and generate visually dramatic modifications. They are located in Adobe Photoshop's Filters tab. Adobe Sensei's machine learning and artificial intelligence engine powers Neural Filters, which use algorithms to add new pixels to your images. This allows you to swiftly experiment with new, creative ideas and make nondestructive changes without compromising the original image.

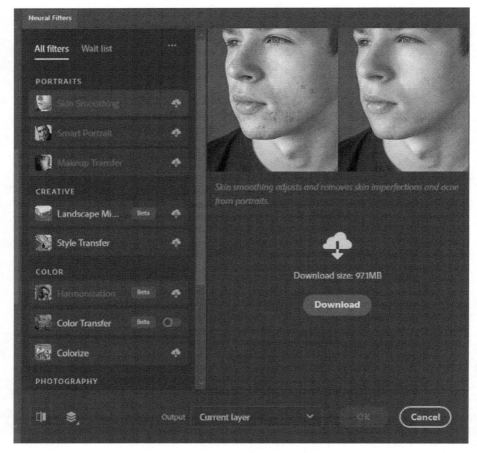

Photoshop comes with five built-in feature filters in the Neural Filters section that you can use as soon as you open your picture. Pick one to make your shot better, or try them all to see which one works best for you.

❖ **Skin Smoothing**: Brushing and adjusting your subjects' skin is made easy with the Skin Smoothing filter. The simple Smoothness and Blur sliders allow you to swiftly erase freckles, scars, tattoos, and other features from faces and skin.

- **Smart Portraits**: This filter's adjustable sliders allow you to change your subject's age, posture, expressions, and any other small details. Make and modify masks that you can use on your subject to evoke strange feelings or even make small aesthetic changes. Use the Retain Unique Details slider to preserve your topic's unique features despite all the changes.
- **Makeup Transfer**: This handy tool allows you to apply the same cosmetics settings to several faces. To achieve the ideal look, add extra makeup to a photo or alter the model's existing makeup entirely in post-production.
- **Landscape Mixer**: Create completely original landscapes by combining the best elements of two pictures. Start with a landscape shot of your own, then select a reference image. To generate a new image, Landscape Mixer will combine elements from the two. To alter how the time of day and season appears, use the Winter, Spring, Summer, Fall, and Sunset sliders.
- **Style Transfer**: As its name suggests, you can use this filter to apply the color, hue, or saturation of one image to another. By changing the Style Strength, Brush Size, and Blur Background sliders and checking the boxes for Preserve Color and Focus Subject, you may choose how much of the final look your image has.
- **Harmonization**: As you work with the sliders and apply a mask, take in the symmetry of the colors as the Harmonization filter applies the color and tone of your reference image to any layer.
- **Color Transfer**: Beautiful colors move fluidly from one picture to the next in a handful of seconds. Use Color Transfer to apply the color scheme from any reference image to the chosen photo. Try with various color moods, experiment with the infinite number of reference photo possibilities, and add a new perspective to old photos.
- **Colorize**: With this option, you can quickly convert black and white images to vivid colors. Select the colors you want to see in your photo, and Adobe Sensei will add those colors to the image. Focus points allow you to apply additional color to certain areas of the filter to fine-tune it.
- **Super Zoom**: Concentrate intently on one thing while keeping the details clear. To minimize noise, eliminate compression artifacts, improve face features, and let your subject—whatever it is—shine through in an extreme close-up.
- **Depth Blur**: Your photo will be blurry by default. Adjust as needed, add some haze, and mask out the foreground. Use Photoshop's preset sliders to change the amount of haze as well as its color temperature, hue, saturation, and other elements.

- ✥ **JPEG Artifacts Removal**: The more times you save a JPEG file, the more likely it is that your image may appear pixelated or fuzzy. Artifacts, or noticeable visual imperfections, may be observed as a result of the compression algorithms used to reduce the file size. By altering the blur level at the edge of the image from high to medium to low, you may use this filter to reverse the process and refine it.
- ✥ **Photo Restoration**: There is a photo restoration feature in Photoshop Beta. Adobe announced in June 2022. It recovers outdated or damaged photos using a novel neural filter driven by artificial intelligence. By using extra adjustments or simple editing tools, you can refine them even more. These sliders are all easy to use.

Filter Gallery
You can obtain a preview of an image's appearance after applying a particular filter in the Filter Gallery. Instead of having to apply numerous filters to an image one at a time, you may preview the effect through the gallery.

Before you click on a filter to receive a preview, you can see an icon that illustrates what the filter does and how it will appear on your image. This can speed up and simplify the process of finding a filter or the particular kind of filter you're looking for. Additionally, you can modify the filter's settings in the Filter Gallery before applying them to your image.

Adaptive Wide Angle
Use an adaptive wide-angle filter to correct lens distortions caused by using wide-angle lenses. It is easy to straighten lines that appear bent in panoramas and images taken with wide-angle and fish-eye lenses. For example, when taken with a wide-angle lens, structures seem to be leaning inward.

After identifying the camera and lens models, the filter uses the lens's attributes to align the images. Use several limitations to draw attention to straight lines in different parts of the picture. Using this information, the Adaptive Wide-Angle filter removes the distortions.

You may also use this filter on images without camera and lens information, however it would take a bit more effort. To change the filter parameters later, turn the layer into a smart object.

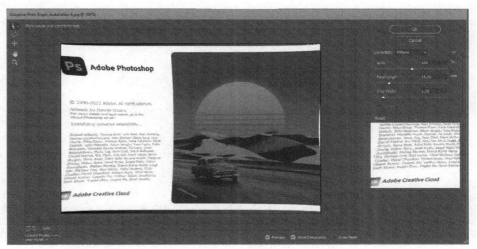

Camera Raw Filter

Originally developed as an Adobe Bridge plug-in, Camera Raw allowed photographers to work on their unprocessed images without having to spend a lot of money on pricey editing software. Since then, Camera Raw has evolved into a powerful image editor in its own right, upon which Lightroom's image processing capabilities have been built. Instead of using more common picture modifications like Curves or Hue/Saturation, users have also had the option to use Camera Raw as a filter on RGB or greyscale photographs from the first edition of Photoshop CC.

The Camera Raw filter can only be applied to greyscale or RGB photos with a maximum pixel count of 65,000 in each dimension. Press the Command + Shift + A keyboard shortcut on a Mac or the Control + Shift + A keyboard shortcut on a PC to select the Camera Raw Filter option from the Filter menu in Photoshop.

You can make changes to an image without changing the original by converting it from Camera Raw into a Smart Object (Smart Filter) layer.

This lets you adjust the Camera Raw settings, just as you would when working on a raw image. Certain workflows might benefit from this. When working with scanned photos, for example, capture sharpening can be applied using the Camera Raw filter. Maybe you'll be more comfortable using the Camera Raw Basic panel controls for tone-editing an image instead of Levels or Curves.

The ability to apply additional Camera Raw-specific modifications, such as adjusting the mid-tone contrast using Clarity or performing black-and-white conversions in the Camera Raw style, is an extra advantage.

Lens Correction

The Lens Correction filter corrects common lens defects like chromatic aberration, vignetting, barrel and Pincushion distortion, and more. Only greyscale or RGB images with 8 or 16 bits per channel can be processed by the filter.

The filter can also be used to rotate an image and correct perspective issues caused by a tilt of the camera, either vertically or horizontally. Compared to the Transform command, the filter's picture grid makes these adjustments more straightforward and precise.

Photoshop Lens Correction can be used in two different ways. Another option is to let Photoshop do the fixes itself. The issue is that you have no control over the situation. The manual method is therefore a possibility.

Liquify

The Liquify tool is one of Photoshop's best tools for photo editing and repair. With it, you can easily fix problems like distortion or wrinkles, or you may create completely new effects by going beyond simple tweaks.

To start making changes, just select the "liquify" tool from the toolbar. Because there are multiple options, you can customize the impact to achieve the results you want. You can also save your preferences as a preset for later use.

Create unique, striking effects with your photos by experimenting with the liquify tool. Give it a try and see what comes to mind!

Vanishing Point

Vanishing Point facilitates perspective-correct editing of images that include perspective planes, such as the sides of a building, walls, floors, or any rectangular object. Before making any changes, such as painting, cloning, copying or pasting, or distorting, you use

Vanishing Point to define the planes in an image. Every change you make respects the plane you're working on's perspective. Whether you edit, add, or remove content from an image, the results are more realistic because the modifications are appropriately orientated and scaled to the perspective planes. When you're done with Vanishing Point, you can continue working on the image in Photoshop. If you wish to preserve the perspective plane information in an image, save your project in the PSD, TIFF, or JPEG formats.

Let`s quickly examine some of the other filters in the Filer menu.

Artistic Filter
By simulating the appearance of traditional or natural media, these filter effects give pictures a painted or artistic appearance. When filters are applied artistically, color, brushstrokes, and textures are combined to create innovative painted-art images. It is mostly used in fine art or commercial projects and performs effectively.

Artistic Filters include **Colored Pencils, Cutouts, Dry Brush, Film Grain, Fresco, Neon Glow, Paint Daubs, Palette Knife, Plastic Wrap, Poster Edges, Rough Pastels, Smudge Stick, Sponge, Underpainting**, and **Watercolor**.

- **Colored Pencil**: The graphics in this effect have a rough crosshatch appearance because pencil colors are used on a solid background.

- **Cutout**: This option creates an image that exactly resembles the rough-cut bits of colorful paper.

- **Dry Brush**: By limiting its color range to the common color areas, this function gives a dry brush appearance when painting the image's edges.

- **Film Grain**: It can get rid of blend banding and give the shadow tones and mid-tones a more saturated pattern.

- **Smudge Stick**: To soften the darker parts, try applying short diagonal strokes. It can lose detail when applied to lighter areas.

- **Neon Glow**: This option allows you to colorize and soften an image by adding several kinds of lights to it.

- **Palette Knife**: By reducing the visual details, you can create the appearance of a canvas that has been lightly painted.

- **Watercolor**: With this option, the photographs will have a watercolor effect thanks to a medium brush that has been loaded with color and water.

- **Paint Daubs**: The photographs have a painted appearance and users can choose from a variety of brush sizes and types.

- **Plastic Wrap**: For accentuating the surface detail of the image, it creates the appearance of a liquid or slick plastic coating.

295

Blur Filters

It is a collection of filters primarily used in photo editing. It can be applied to the entire image or only a specific portion of it. You can also select the type and degree of blur you want. Blur filters average color, direction, and distance to produce a variety of unique blur effects. These can eliminate undesired dust, noise, and roughness from the image while softening and defocusing it. Additionally, they can be utilized to blend in recently added background elements.

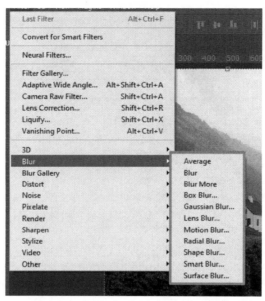

- ✦ **Average**: It will help you find pictures or selections with mediocre colors so you can add your favorite hue to make them look smoother.
- ✦ **Movement Blur**: It is used to improve realistic motion effects. For example, this effect can provide the appearance that an image contains a moving object with a predetermined exposure period.
- ✦ **Shape Blur**: The blur is produced by a kernel, which can be chosen from a selection of form presets. To adjust its size, use the radius slider.
- ✦ **Surface Blur**: With this filter option, you can blur an image without sacrificing its sharp edges. It is usually used to reduce noise and grain in the photos.
- ✦ **Lens blur**: By creating the illusion of a reduced field of view, this filter blurs the background and draws emphasis to the image's important components.
- ✦ **Gaussian Blur**: It provides a configurable amount of blurriness or haze to the chosen area of the image. Additionally, it offers a low-frequency detail.

- **Radial Blur**: By choosing the Spin option and then deciding how far to rotate the camera, you may add a gentle blur to a zoomed-out or spinning image.
- **Smart Blur**: Once you've chosen the ideal threshold, radius, and blur quality, this filter option will allow you to blur the image precisely.

Blur Gallery Filters

The Blur Gallery Filters are an advanced version of the blur filters that provide more intricate, specialized blur patterns and applications. These can produce blur along a path by mimicking the lenses of a normal camera. Drag the checkmarks next to each of the five Blur Gallery filters on the right side of the screen to use them all at once.

Field, Iris, Tilt-Shift, Path, and Spin blur filters are all part of the Blur Gallery Filters.

Brush Strokes Filters

To improve the aesthetic appeal of the images, a number of brush and pen stroke effects are used. You can apply a variety of effects to the pictures with the brush stroke filters, including paint, noise, texture, and edge detail. Brushstroke filters use color, line, and texture to simulate conventional paintbrushes and painting methods.

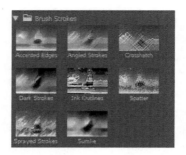

The following brush stroke filters are available: Sumi-e, Spatter, Sprayed Strokes, Dark Strokes, Accented Edges, Angled Strokes, and Crosshatch.

- **Splatter**: This result is comparable to the splatter airbrush effect, which can be utilized to streamline the image's overall effects.
- **Dark Strokes**: You'll be able to paint the lighter sections efficiently with long, white strokes and the darker areas effectively with short, dark strokes.
- **Sprayed Strokes**: By using sprayed and angular strokes using Sprayed, you can repaint a picture using dominant colors.
- **Angles Strokes**: By using sprayed and angular strokes using Sprayed, you can repaint a picture using dominant colors.
- **Crosshatch**: By including approximated pencil hatching, it helps to add texture and roughen the borders of colored sections of an image.

Distort Filters
Distortion filters are used to shift, compress, and stretch pixels to create a variety of effects. Often, these require more computer RAM to function.

Diffuse glow, displacement, glass, ocean ripple, pinch, polar coordinates, ripple, shear, spherize, twist, wave, and zigzag are examples of distortion filters.

- ✦ **Spherize**: By warping the image or selection and bending it to fit the curve, it will create the illusion of three dimensions.
- ✦ **ZigZag**: To accurately distort the selected part of the image, you must specify the radius of the pixel and comprehend how to move it.
- ✦ **Ripple**: In this situation, you must define the dimensions and quantity of ripples based on which an undulating pattern will be produced in the specified area.
- ✦ **Ocean Ripple**: Using it, you can add irregularly spaced ripples to the picture's surface to give the impression that it is underwater.
- ✦ **Glass**: This effect gives the impression that you are wearing various types of glasses to watch the image. You can apply it or make your glass effect.
- ✦ **Displace**: With this effect, the image appears to be seen through several types of glasses. You can utilize it or make your customized glass effect to apply

Noise Filters

Noise filters either add or remove noise, which is the erratic color or brightness of image pixels, to create a more consistent image or texture.

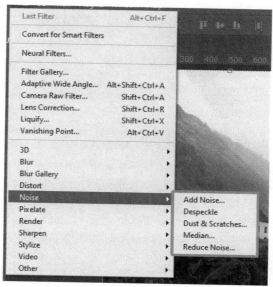

- ✦ **Reduce Noise**: By lowering the noise and maintaining the edges, it will have an impact on the image as a whole or the specific choices.

- **Add Noise**: You may give photographs that have been heavily edited a realistic appearance by adding ransom pixels.
- **Dust & Scratches**: In this situation, you can lessen the noise and strike a balance between intensifying the image and hiding imperfections.
- **Median**: To lessen noise, it combines the pixel brightness inside the selection. The filter can also be used to lessen motion effects.

Pixelate Filters

These filter sets are used to define a selection by grouping cells with pixels of the same color. Pixelate Filters combine colors to create effects and patterns.

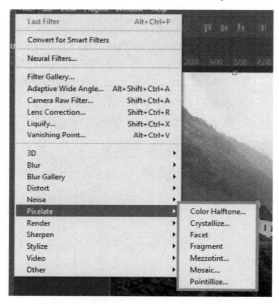

- **Color Halftone**: It gives the impression that the image is divided into rectangles and then replaced on each channel of a bigger halftone screen.
- **Facet**: When this effect is present, solid or similar-colored pixels will cluster together to form blocks of the same color. It is typically employed to give the scanned image a hand-painted appearance.
- **Mezzotint**: Using this filter, you can change a normal image into a random black-and-white pattern or highly saturated hues into a color image.
- **Pointillize**: In this type of effect, you can disperse the colors of the image into haphazardly scattered dots, much like in a pointillist painting.

Render Filters

This filter can create a wide variety of 3D shapes, including spherical, cubical, and cylindrical shapes, as well as various cloud patterns, lighting effects, and refraction and reflection patterns. Render filters produce new pictures that can be combined with or used in lieu of preexisting ones. Tree, Clouds, Picture Frame, Flame, and Distinction Render filters include things like clouds, fibers, lens flare, and lighting effects (deprecated (3D).

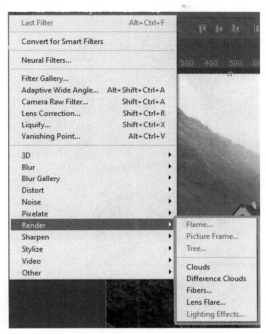

✦ **Clouds**: By utilizing random values that fluctuate between background and foreground colors, it is possible to produce a gentle cloud pattern.

✦ **Lighting Effects**: By adjusting various styles, types, and characteristics, you can use this filter to generate an infinite number of lighting effects on RGB photographs.

✦ **Fibers**: This filter uses the color of the foreground and background to simulate woven fibers in the image.

✦ **Lens flare**: In this situation, shining a strong light through the camera lens will make it appear as though there is refraction occurring inside the image.

Stylize Filters

The pixels will move and the contrast will rise as a result of this effect, giving the chosen image a painted appearance. Stylized filters produce dynamic embossing and line-art effects by adding depth, height, and line effects.

Examples of stylized filters include Diffuse, Emboss, Extrude, Find Edges, Glowing Edges, Oil Paint, Solarize, Tiles, Trace Contour, and Wind.

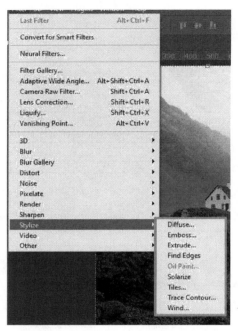

✦ **Diffuse**: By rearranging the pixels in the selection by various settings like normal, lighten only, darken only, etc., you can use it to soften the focus.

✦ **Wind**: The photographs can have a wind-blown appearance thanks to this filter. It offers many options including Wind, Blast, and Stagger.

✦ **Find Edges**: This effect will highlight the edges of the image and assist you in locating the specific areas of the image that have undergone various alterations.

✦ **Tiles**: The image can be divided into a sequence of tiles, with the space between each tile able to be filled with a variety of alternatives, including the reversed image, the foreground color, the background color, the original image, etc.

✦ **Glowing Edges**: This technique may be used cumulatively by locating the color edges of the photos and incorporating a neon-like glow into them.

Sharpen Filters

To improve the edges of photographs and produce sharper, more distinct lines and separation, sharpening filters use contrast.

In order to improve the edges of photographs and produce sharper, more distinct lines and separation, sharpening filters use contrast.

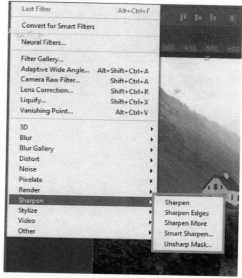

Sharpen Filters include Sharpen, Sharpen Edges, Sharpen More, Smart Sharpen, and Unsharp Mask.

Video Filters

Frames from or for videos are processed using video filters.

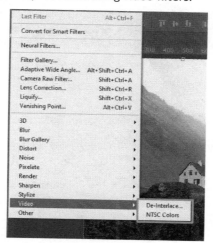

Video Filters include De-Interlace and NTSC Colors.

Other Filters

You can modify the photo masks, balance the image selection, change the colors, and make your own filters by selecting "Others" from this sub-menu. In addition to making custom filters, you may use other filters to swiftly move and alter pixels.

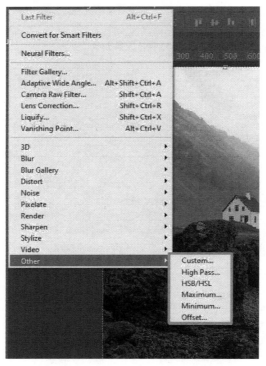

Other Filters include Custom, High Pass, HSB/HSL, Material Filter, Maximum, Minimum, and Offset.

Maximum and Minimum: These are used to modify masks. The "Maximum" filter will give the effect of a spread whereas the "Minimum" filter will give the effect of a choke.

Custom: Using this option, you can customize your effect and adjust the brightness of each pixel according to convolution, that is, a predefined mathematical operation.

High Pass: This effect will help you retain the image edges according to the specified radius while allowing you to conceal the rest. It`s just the opposite of the Gaussian blur.

CHAPTER ELEVEN

TIPS AND TRICKS ON PHOTOSHOP 2025

- **How to use Photoshop's Preference Window to adjust settings.**
- **Shortcuts for Blending Modes.**
- **How to load and save Photoshop choices.**
- **Common Photoshop shortcuts.**
- **Shortcuts to the tools for selecting.**
- **Shortcuts for Function Keys.**
- **Shortcuts for object selection and moving objects.**
- **Text selection and editing shortcuts**

Tips and Tricks

In this section, we'll cover some useful Photoshop tips and tricks. Photoshop tips and tricks are provided to encourage a culture of using the application.

Let's now examine some amazing Photoshop 2025 techniques and tricks.

The Preference Window

Photoshop offers a wide range of customization choices. In addition to altering how its tools behave and how your workspace looks, the software's settings, which control many aspects of Photoshop, let you turn features on or off, modify how tools behave, and fine-tune how the application runs.

In Windows, you can find your **preference** in **Edit** the **Menu Bar** while in the macOS, choose **Photoshop> Preferences** to open the preferences dialog box.

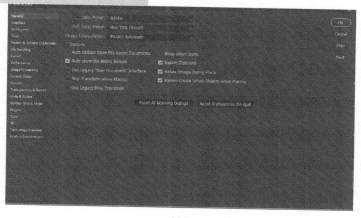

Most of our tips and techniques will be taught using the Preference dialogue box.

To customize your Photoshop Interface do the following,

- Make the required adjustments by clicking on Interface on the left side of the window dialogue box after gaining access to your Preference dialogue box.

To change the ruler unit of measurement, do the following,

- Photoshop offers a wide range of measurement units, including pixels, inches, centimeters, millimeters, points, picas, and percentages. Make sure that the ruler is visible before adjusting the unit of measurement; if not, select **Ruler** from the **View menu** in the **Menu bar.**
- After the ruler displays at the top and left of your image, right-click anywhere on it to get a pop-up menu where you can choose the desired unit of measurement.

Or

- Choose **Unit** & **Rulers** from the Preference window dialogue box.
- Select a different unit of measurement in the window that follows.

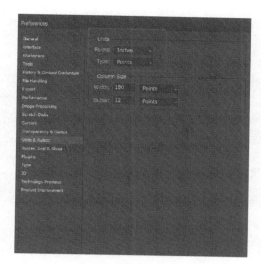

To change the appearance of your brush tips during usage, do the below,

- ✤ Click on Cursor after navigating to your preference preferences, then make your changes in the window that displays.

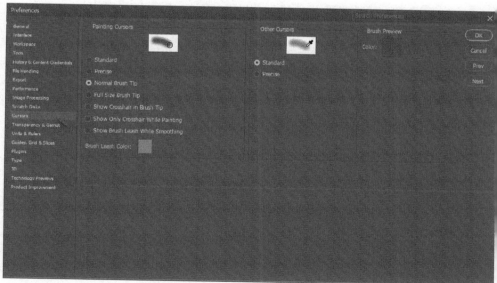

To search and find your required preferences, do the following,

- ✤ To open the Preferences dialog, use **Cmd/Ctrl** + **K** on the keyboard.

- Now, use the Preferences dialog's search feature by pressing **Cmd/Ctrl** + **F** on your keyboard.
- Your result is the image below.

Preference to improve Selection Stability

Some Photoshop desktop users on Windows were experiencing slow performance, crashes, or unexpected selections because of NVidia Windows Display drivers. The app's performance has been adjusted for Windows users who are having these issues. Use the steps below to increase the selection stability.

- To open the Preferences dialog, use **Cmd/Ctrl** + **K**
- Select **Image Processing** on the left side of the **Preferences dialog.**
- For Selections Processing, toggle from **Faster** to **More Stable**

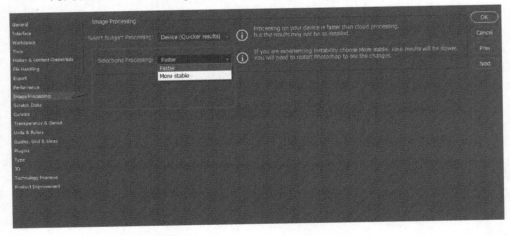

Shortcuts for blending modes

Shortcut Result	Windows	macOS
Switch between blending modes.	Shift + + (plus) or – (minus)	Shift + + (plus) or – (minus)
To use the Normal mode	Shift + Alt + N	Shift + Option + N

To use the Dissolve mode	Shift + Alt + I	Shift + Option + I
To use the Behind Mode (brush tool only)	Shift + Alt + Q	Shift + Option + Q
To use the Clear Mode (Brush Tool Only)	Shift + Alt + R	Shift + Option + R
To use the Darken mode	Shift + Alt + K	Shift + Option + K
To use the Multiply mode	Shift + Alt + M	Shift + Option + M
To use the Color Burn mode	Shift + Alt + B	Shift + Option + B
To use the Linear Burn mode	Shift + Alt + A	Shift + Option + A
To use the Lighten mode	Shift + Alt + G	Shift + Option + G
To use the Screen mode	Shift + Alt + S	Shift + Option + S
To use the Color Dodge mode	Shift + Alt + D	Shift + Option + D
To use the Linear Dodge mode	Shift + Alt + W	Shift + Option + W
To use the Overlay mode	Shift + Alt + O	Shift + Option + O
To use the Soft Light mode	Shift + Alt + F	Shift + Option + F
To use the Hard Light mode	Shift + Alt + H	Shift + Option + H
To use the Vivid Light mode	Shift + Alt + V	Shift + Option + V
To use the Linear Light mode	Shift + Alt + J	Shift + Option + J
To use the Pin Light mode	Shift + Alt + Z	Shift + Option + Z
To use the Hard Mix mode	Shift + Alt + L	Shift + Option + L
To use the Difference mode	Shift + Alt + E	Shift + Option + E
To use the Exclusion mode	Shift + Alt + X	Shift + Option + X
To use the Hue mode	Shift + Alt + U	Shift + Option + U
To use the Saturation mode	Shift + Alt + T	Shift + Option + T
To use the Color mode	Shift + Alt + C	Shift + Option + C
To use the Luminosity mode	Shift + Alt + Y	Shift + Option + Y
To use the Desaturate mode	Sponge tool + Shift + Alt + D	Sponge tool + Shift + Alt + D
To use the Saturate mode	Sponge tool + Shift + Alt + S	Sponge tool + Shift + Option + S

To apply the Dodge/Burn Shadows	Dodge tool/Burn tool + Shift + Alt + S	Dodge tool/Burn tool + Shift + Option + S
To apply the Dodge/Burn Mid-tones	Dodge tool/Burn tool + Shift + Alt + M	Dodge tool/Burn tool + Shift + Option + M
To apply Dodge/Burn Highlights	Dodge tool/Burn tool + Shift + Alt + H	Dodge tool/Burn tool + Shift + Option + H

Saving Selections in Photoshop

Saving the choice will be a simpler method to relieve the tension that comes with having to make the same choice repeatedly. To save selections in Photoshop, adhere to the guidelines provided below.

- ✦ Make your selection.
- ✦ Select **Save Selection** from the **Select Menu** in the Menu Bar

- ✦ Name your selection then click **OK** to save your selection

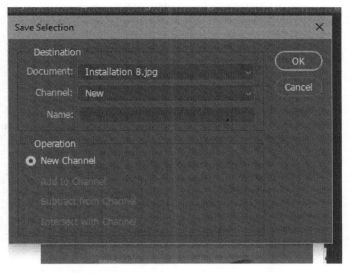

Loading Selections in Photoshop

Only saved selections can be loaded in Photoshop, Follow the instructions below to load your saved selections in Photoshop.

✦ From the **Select Menu** in the **Menu Bar**, Click on **Load Selection.**

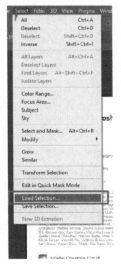

✦ Select your saved selection and click **OK** to reopen it.

Popular Shortcuts in Photoshop

Shortcut Result	Windows	macOS
Free Transform	Control + T	Command + T
Toggle between painting and erasing with the same brush	Hold down~ (tilde accent)	Hold down~ (tilde accent)
Deselect Selections	Control + D	Command + D
Undo Last Command	Control + Z	Command + Z
Decrease Brush Size	[	[
Increase Brush Size	]	]
Decrease Brush Hardness	{	{
Increase Brush Hardness	}	}
Rotate the brush tip by 1 degree	Left Arrow (anti-clockwise), Right Arrow (clockwise)	Left Arrow (anti-clockwise), Right Arrow (clockwise)
Rotate the brush tip by 15 degrees	Shift + Left Arrow (anti-clockwise), Shift + Right Arrow (clockwise)	Shift + Left Arrow (anti-clockwise), Shift + Right Arrow (clockwise)
Default Foreground/Background	D	D
Switch Foreground/ Background	X	X
Fit layer(s) to screen	Alt-click layer	Option-click layer

Fit all to Screen	Alt + 0	Option + 0
New layer via copy	Control + J	Command + J
New layer via cut	Shift + Control + J	Shift + Command + J
Add to a selection	Any selection tool + Shift-drag	Any selection tool + Shift-drag
Delete Brush or Swatch	Alt-click brush or swatch	Option-click brush or swatch
With the Move tool chosen, turn on the auto-select checkbox in the Options bar.	Control-click	Command-click (Hold the Command key)
Close all open documents other than the current document	Ctrl + Alt + P	Command + Option + P
Cancel any modal dialog window (including the Start Workspace)	Escape	Escape
Choose the toolbar's first edit field.	Enter	Return
Move around the fields	Tab	Tab
Change the direction of your navigation between the fields.	Tab + Shift	Tab + Shift
Replacing Cancel with Reset	Alt	Option

Function Keys Shortcuts

Shortcut Result	Windows	macOS
Start Help	F1	Help Key
Undo/Redo		F1
Cut	F2	F2
Copy	F3	F3
Paste	F4	F4
Show/Hide Brush Panel	F5	F5
Show/Hide Color Panel	F6	F6
Show/Hide Layer panel	F7	F7
Show/Hide Info Panel	F8	F8
Show/Hide Actions Panel	F9	Option + F9
Revert	F12	F12

Fill	Shift + F5	Shift + F5
Feather Selection	Shift + F6	Shift + F6
Inverse Selection	Shift + F7	Shift + F7

Shortcuts for Selection Tools

Shortcuts Result	Window	macOS
Use the same shortcut key to switch between tools.	Shift-press shortcut key (if Use Shift Key for Tool Switch preference is selected)	Shift-press shortcut key (if Use Shift Key for Tool Switch preference is selected)
Go through all the hidden tools	Alt-click + tool (except Add Anchor Point, Delete Anchor Point, and Convert Point tools)	Option-click + tool (except Add Anchor Point, Delete Anchor Point, and Convert Point tools)
Move tool Artboard tool	V	V
Rectangular Marquee tool Elliptical Marquee tool	M	M
Lasso tool Polygonal Lasso tool Magnetic Lasso tool	L	L
Object Selection tool Quick Selection tool Magic Wand tool	W	W
Crop tool Perspective Crop tool Slice tool Slice Select tool	C	C
Eyedropper tool Color Sampler tool Ruler tool Note tool	I	I
Frame tool	K	K
Eyedropper tool 3D Material Eyedropper tool (ADD) Color Sampler tool Ruler tool Note tool	I	I

Count tool		
Spot Healing Brush tool	J	J
Healing Brush tool		
Patch tool		
Red Eye tool		
Content-Aware Move tool		
Red Eye tool		
Brush tool	B	B
Pencil tool		
Color Replacement tool		
Mixer Brush tool		
Clone Stamp tool	S	S
Pattern Stamp tool		
History Brush tool	Y	Y
Art History Brush tool		
Eraser tool	E	E
Background Eraser tool		
Magic Eraser tool		
Gradient tool	G	G
Paint Bucket tool		
3D Material Drop tool		
Dodge too	O	O
Burn tool		
Sponge tool		
Pen tool	P	P
Freeform Pen tool		
Curvature Pen tool		
Horizontal Type tool	T	T
Vertical Type tool		
Horizontal Type mask tool		
Vertical Type mask tool		
Path Selection tool	A	A
Direct Selection tool		
Rectangle tool	U	U
Ellipse tool		
Polygon tool		
Line tool		
Custom Shape tool		
Hand tool	H	H

Rotate View tool	R	R
Zoom tool	Z	Z
Liquify		
Toggle Standard/Quick Mask modes	Q	Q
Toggle Preserve Transparency	/	/
Previous Brush	,	,
Next Brush	.	.
First Brush	<	<
Last Brush	>	>

Shortcuts for viewing images

Shortcut Result	Windows	macOS
Go through open documents	Control + Tab	Command + Tab
Return to previous document	Shift + Control + Tab	Shift + Command + (grave accent)
Shut off a Photoshop file and launch Bridge.	Shift-Control-W	Shift-Command-W
Switch forward between Standard screen mode, Full-screen mode with menu bar, and Full-screen mode	F	F
Switch (back) between the following modes: Standard screen mode, Full-screen mode with menu bar, and Full-screen mode.	Shift + F	Shift + F
Forward-swiping canvas color	Spacebar + F (or right-click canvas background and select color)	Spacebar + F (or Control-click canvas background and select color)
Toggle the canvas's color backward.	Spacebar + Shift + F	Spacebar + Shift + F
Fit image in window	Double-click Hand tool	Double-click Hand tool
Magnify 100%	Double-click Zoom tool or Ctrl + 1	Double-click Zoom tool or Command + 1

Change to a hand tool (when not in text-edit mode)	Spacebar	Spacebar
Pan numerous documents at once with the Hand tool.	Shift-drag	Shift-drag
Switch to Zoom In tool	Control + spacebar	Command + spacebar
Use the Zoom Out tool now.	Alt + spacebar	Option + spacebar
Drag the Zoom tool while moving the Zoom marquee.	Spacebar-drag	Spacebar-drag
Keep the zoom percentage box open when applying the zoom percentage.	Shift + Enter to zoom in or out of the Navigator panel.	Use Shift + Return to zoom in or out of the Navigator panel.
Specified portion of an image is zoomed in	Control-drag the Navigator panel's preview.	Command-drag over the Navigator panel's preview
To Temporarily zoom into an image	Click the image while holding down the mouse button while holding down H.	Click the image while holding down the mouse button while holding down H.
Image scrolling using a hand tool	Drag the view area box in the Navigator panel using the spacebar.	Drag the view area box in the Navigator panel using the spacebar.
To Scroll up or down 1 screen	Page Up or Page Down	Page Up or Page Down
Scroll ten units up or down.	Page Down or Page Up with Shift	Page Down or Page Up with Shift
View can be moved to the upper-left or lower-right corner.	Home or End	Home or End
As Rubylith, toggle layer mask on and off (layer mask must be selected)	\ (backslash)	\ (backslash)

Shortcut for selecting and moving objects

Shortcut Result	Windows	macOS
Move the marquee while selecting	Any marquee tool + spacebar drag (apart from	Any marquee tool + spacebar drag (apart from

	single column and single row)	single column and single row)
Add to a selection	Any selection tool + Shift-drag	Any selection tool + Shift-drag
Take away from a selection	Any selection tool + Alt-drag	Any selection tool + Option-drag
Intersect a selection	Shift-Alt-Drag plus any selection tool (apart from the Quick Selection tool)	Shift-Option-drag plus any selection tool (apart from the Quick Selection tool)
Draw a marquee from the center (if no other selections are active)	Alt-drag	Option-drag
Change to the Lasso tool from the Magnetic Lasso tool	Alt-drag	Option-drag
Use the polygonal Lasso tool instead of the Magnetic Lasso tool.	Alt-click	Option-click
Widening/narrowing the detection window	Magnetic Lasso tool + [or]	Magnetic Lasso tool + [or]
Whether to accept cropping or not	Enter or Esc + Crop Tool	Crop tool + Backspace or Esc
(Except when View > Snap is unchecked) Snap guide to ruler ticks	Shift-drag guide	Shift-drag guide
change the direction of the horizontal or vertical guide	Alt-drag guide	Option-drag guide

Shortcuts for Selecting and editing texts

Shortcuts Result	Windows	macOS
Change the type in an image	When the Type layer is selected, control-drag type.	When the Type layer is selected, command-drag the type.
Choose 1 word left/right, 1 line down/up, or 1 character left/right.	Down Arrow/Up Arrow, Shift + Left/Right Arrow, or Control + Shift + Left/Right Arrow	Command + Shift + Left/Right Arrow or Down/Up Arrow, or Shift + Left/Right Arrow

Select characters from insertion point to the mouse click point	Shift-click	Shift-click
Move 1 word left/right, 1 line up/down, or 1 character left/right	Arrows to the left or right, up or down, or control while using the left or right arrows	Down/Up Arrows, Left/Right Arrows, or Command + Left/Right Arrows
To create a new text layer when a text layer is chosen in the Layers panel,	Shift-click	Shift-click
Choose a phrase, line, paragraph, or short tale.	Double-click, triple-click, four-click, five-click, etc.	Double-click, triple-click, four-click, five-click, etc.
show/hide the specified type's selection	Control + H	Command + H
When changing the bounding box's size, scale the text inside of it.	Control-drag a box handle to move it.	You may command-drag a bounding box handle.
To move the text box while creating a text box,	Spacebar-drag	Spacebar-drag

Troubleshooting in Photoshop

Photoshop is unquestionably one of Adobe's enhanced products with special features. However, one or two problems will arise.

I will address a number of issues you may face and provide solutions in this section of the chapter.

Issues	Solutions
Using the Select Subject or Object Selection Tool causes [Win] to crash. The Select and Mask and Object Selection tools are unavailable, and the Photoshop application crashes.	Use the official website to update your Nvidia drivers.
When you run Photoshop, it either freezes during setup or at the splash screen that reads "Loading Halide Bottlenecks..."	First, download the most recent version of Photoshop. If making the updates do not solve the problem then remove any large custom preset file.
To remove large custom preset files.	◆ Hold down the Option key when choosing Library from the Go menu in the Finder. Go to

	Preferences > Adobe Photoshop > Version Year > Settings. ♦ Look for the preset files with a significant file size in the Settings folder. Such preset files should be relocated from the Settings folder to a short-term location (for example, a new folder on your desktop).
When opening new documents, a green screen issue occurs. When you open a new blank document or an existing document in Photoshop 24.0, a green screen flickers in the background.	To get around this, take the following actions: ♦ Disable the Use Graphics Processor option under Preferences > Performance. ♦ restart Photoshop
Not recognizing the picture size copied to the clipboard The New Document dialog does not recognize the right image dimensions transferred to the clipboard when creating a new document with an image in it.	Check the Creative Cloud desktop app for updates. ♦ Click Check for Updates under the "Updates" tab in the Creative Cloud Desktop software. ♦ Try logging out and back into the Creative Cloud desktop app to see if that fixes the issue.
In the Save As dialog box, the Save button is inactive or non-responsive. After the macOS 12.3 update, Photoshop's Save As dialog box no longer has a working save button.	The Save button will become active once more if you slightly resize the save window.
Photoshop launches slowly (Win only) Photoshop may take a while to launch on your Windows machine.	Workaround: Take the following actions: ♦ Your **Windows Image Acquisition** (WIA) settings need to be restarted ♦ Change **Startup Type** from "**Automatic**" to "**Automatic (Delayed Start)**" in WIA attributes.
If you utilize Nvidia G-SYNC, Photoshop mouse stuttering may be an issue for you.	Take any of the following actions as a workaround: ♦ Enter the Nvidia **Control Panel** > **3D Settings** > **Manage 3D Settings** to disable G-SYNC for Photoshop.

Scroll down to **Monitor Technology**, choose **Fixed Refresh** from the dropdown option, and then click Apply after selecting Photoshop from the **Program Settings** tab.

⇕ Select **Technology Previews** > **Preferences** > and turn on **Deactivate Native Canvas**. Start Photoshop again.

Photoshop won't accept desktop photos from Lightroom Masks may need to be recalculated in Adobe Camera Raw when importing JPEG, HEIC, TIFF, PNG, and PSD files of pictures edited in Lightroom desktop to the Photoshop home screen. The masks may not always be found in their original shape.	If your Lightroom desktop photo masks cannot be recovered by Adobe Camera Raw, you can: ‡ Lightroom exports images to your local machine. ‡ Select Edit in Photoshop from the export option in Lightroom.

Photoshop unable to explore in Bridge
When you choose **File** > **Browse In Bridge** from within Photoshop, Bridge does not launch.
	Workaround: Take the following actions:
	‡ Remove Photoshop and Bridge from your computer.
	‡ Rename the following database folders:
	   o C:\Program Files (x86)\Common Files\Adobe\Adobe PCD
	   o C:\Program Files (x86)\Common Files\Adobe\caps
	‡ Install Bridge and Photoshop once more after removing them in Step 1.
	Using the Alt+Tab keys, you may also try switching from Photoshop to Bridge. On Mac ARM, though, this is not supported.

CONCLUSION

Congratulations on finishing the User's Guide for Adobe Photoshop 2025. You can use some more advanced techniques now that you understand the basics of image editing. You may now begin creating your stunning images with Photoshop.

Here are some guidelines to help you get started.

Practice makes perfect. The more you use Photoshop, the more proficient you will become. Try to set aside some time each day to improve your skills.

Take a test. Do not be afraid to take chances and experiment with Photoshop. There are no rules, so have fun and see what you can think up.

Make use of resources. Numerous materials are available to help you learn Photoshop. There are tutorials, books, websites, and even online courses accessible.

Never give up. Photoshop can be challenging to learn, but the work is definitely worth it. With practice, you will be able to produce amazing photographs using Photoshop.

I hope this book has been helpful to you. Please do not hesitate to contact me with any questions or feedback.

Enjoy the editing process!

INDEX

Z